Own the Zone

"Don Casey, a long-time member of the NBA family who has traveled the world teaching the fundamentals of basketball to all players alike, does an extraordinary job illustrating the key concepts of zone defense. The knowledge and insight he shares are sure to help coaches at all levels."

DAVID J. STERN
NBA Commissioner

"Don Casey is the master of the zone defense in basketball. In his book, *Own the Zone*, Coach Casey not only thoroughly describes principles of zone defense and how to use them, but also shows how to effectively attack zones on offense. *Own the Zone* will become a coach's 'bible.'"

DR. JACK RAMSAY
Hall of Fame coach
ESPN basketball analyst

"When Don Casey was with us at Notre Dame, we incorporated the *Temple of Zones'* 2-3 slides and went to the NCAA tournament. Casey is one of the best 'Xs' and 'Os' people the game ever had."

DIGGER PHELPS
Former head coach, Notre Dame
ESPN basketball analyst

"Zone defense is the real equalizer, but Coach Casey has tipped the scales in favor of the defense for over 40 years. *Own the Zone* gives insight into the defensive slides for victory and informs on how to approach and attack the zone itself. Reading this treasure of knowledge will weaken your opponents."

HOWARD GARFINKEL
Author of *Five-Star Basketball Drills*

"Finally, a book to tell us not just what to do but how to do it. Don't miss this one from Don Casey, the 'Wizard of Zones,' a comprehensive book that will surely become a classic in the U.S. as well as abroad. I recommend it highly."

GIORGIO GANDOLFI
Executive Publisher,
FIBA Assist magazine

"Any young aspiring youth coach, high school coach, or college coach should invest in the purchase of this illustrated book on zone defense. I have never read another zone defensive philosophy that defines positions, responsibilities, and part method disciplines that will enable any team in the world of basketball to implement successfully throughout the season."

TOM NEWELL
FIBA instructor for Olympic Solidarity Programs
Former NBA assistant coach
Former Japan men's national coach
Former WNBA assistant coach

"The basketball world has been waiting for this book."

JAMES FOSTER
Head women's coach,
Ohio State University

"Representing all of the NBA head and assistant coaches as well as our distinguished coaching alumni, The National Basketball Coaches Association is proud of Coach Don Casey and his collaborator, Ralph Pim, for their efforts to bring this useful teaching tool, covering all the aspects of the zone defense, to coaches at all levels. It has always been part of the Association's mission to share our members' knowledge and passion for the game with their peers around the globe. Coaches everywhere and on every level will use this easy-to-follow guide to improve their 'W' column."

MICHAEL GOLDBERG
Executive Director,
National Basketball Coaches Association

"When I want to know something about any zone defense, I contact Don Casey! I don't care if it's zone offense, zone defense, the 2-3, the 3-2, the 2-1-2, or the match-up, I contact Don Casey! He is all things in one when it comes to zones: The Man, The Guru, The Source, The Godfather. Yes, I like 'The Godfather.' I was having trouble with the 3-2 zone in 1979–80 here in Italy. I contacted Don Casey and he gave me the basis of the offense I used from that day forward with great success. So, he knows the zone at both ends of the floor. Like I said, The Godfather!"

DAN PETERSON
Former head coach, University of Delaware
Former head coach, Chilean national team
Former head coach, Olimpia Milano

OWN THE ZONE

EXECUTING AND ATTACKING ZONE DEFENSES

COACH DON CASEY AND **RALPH PIM**

New York   Chicago   San Francisco   Lisbon   London   Madrid   Mexico City
Milan   New Delhi   San Juan   Seoul   Singapore   Sydney   Toronto

Library of Congress Cataloging in Publication Data

Casey, Don, coach.
   Own the zone / by Don Casey and Ralph Pim.
       p.   cm.
     ISBN-13: 978-0-07-148160-1 (alk. paper)
     ISBN-10: 0-07-148160-5 (alk. paper)
      1. Basketball—Defense.   2. Basketball—Coaching.   I. Pim, Ralph L.
  II. Title.
  GV888.C37   2008
  796.323'2—dc22   2007027438

For Dwynne,
LeeAnn, Michael, Sean,
and the little guys—Jack and Alex
DC

To my parents, Alice and Lorin Pim,
who provided a strong foundation, built on integrity, trust,
and respect. You encouraged me to pursue my dreams and were
always there every step of the way.
You are missed dearly.
To my wife, Linda, who is the love of my life and
provides peace and happiness every day. I treasure our time together.
Thanks for your patience and understanding during many
long days of writing Own the Zone.
RP

1 2 3 4 5 6 7 8 9 10 11 12 13 14 15 16 17 18 19 20 DOC/DOC 0 9 8 7

ISBN 978-0-07-148160-1
MHID   0-07-148160-5

Photos in Chapters 4, 6, 8, and 9 are courtesy of Marquette University.
Photos in Chapter 7 are courtesy of Notre Dame College Prep in Niles, Illinois.

McGraw-Hill books are available at special quantity discounts to use as premiums and sales promotions, or for use in corporate training programs. For more information, please write to the Director of Special Sales, Professional Publishing, McGraw-Hill, Two Penn Plaza, New York, NY 10121-2298. Or contact your local bookstore.

This book is printed on acid-free paper.

Contents

Foreword

Don Casey has had a long, successful, and illustrious career as a basketball coach at all levels. Starting out as the coach of Bishop Eustace Preparatory School, he won two back-to-back New Jersey state championships then moved on to be an assistant under Hall of Fame Coach Harry Litwak at Temple University. Don took over the program at Temple, and the team was consistently in the top tier of NCAA defensive stats. Don was then sought out by the NBA's Chicago Bulls as an assistant coach, joining the team in 1982. This led to head and assistant coach assignments with the Boston Celtics, Los Angeles Clippers, and New Jersey Nets.

Whatever level of the game he has coached, Don and his players have utilized the zone defense to great advantage. With the publication of *Own the Zone*, Don and his coauthor, Dr. Ralph Pim, Division Chief of Competitive Sports at West Point, share with basketball coaches around the globe their insights and the wisdom of utilizing the zone defense as a great equalizer and a tactical strategy to keep teams at all levels in the game and poised to win.

Using the techniques set out in *Own the Zone*, coaches at every level will learn how to disrupt and limit superior offenses, create opportunities for their own offense, keep their team in striking distance and build cohesion and chemistry among their players as they work closely on learning this defense.

Don and Ralph have reached out to some of the great early pioneers of the zone defense as well as international coaching greats to provide their zone secrets. There has never been published for the sport of basketball a more thorough, dynamic, and useful defensive tool for coaches at every level than *Own the Zone*. As a basketball coach for over 40 years, I know that this book will help every coach stay in the game, build a team that is active and involved in the game, and more often than not notch a 'W.'"

HUBIE BROWN
Naismith Memorial
Basketball Hall of Famer

Preface

Prepare to Own the Zone

Anyone can play man—for they all do.
ANONYMOUS

Approximately 25 years ago, coauthor Casey wrote a popular book entitled *The Temple of Zones*, which helped coaches understand and employ zone defenses. It is time to expand *The Temple of Zones* with updated offensive and defensive facts that will ensure success in today's basketball world.

Before embarking, it is important to identify the outcome goals of our expedition. *Own the Zone* was written for coaches who want to gain knowledge and help their teams reach their full potential. The lessons learned from *Own the Zone* will

- unlock the secrets of the zone defense.
- identify the key defensive concepts for success.
- introduce an easy-to-follow system for teaching zone defense.
- provide strategies to stop any zone offense.
- identify the key offensive concepts for success.
- create opportunities for teams to win championships.

As Coach Casey has often said: Only a few teach and play zone. *Welcome to the few.*

Acknowledgments

In one's coaching journey, help and guidance are usually needed along the way; if not from the start to the finish. Coauthor Coach Don Casey was fortunate that the Big Five and the Palestra were minutes away from his high school, providing him access not only to games but to Penn, Temple, and St. Joe's practices. Great games and great coaching minds were made available to all those interested, Coach Casey included. Over the years several stand out and he would like to acknowledge them.

The key objective for any assistant coach is to aid in directing the team where the head coach wants to take them. To my assistants at Bishop Eustace Prep (Ralph Bandivoglio, Henry Hurst, Bill Schillig, Joe O'Connor, Bob Degnan), and at Temple University (Jim Maloney, John McCarthy, Tim Brocchi, Jay Norman, Joe O'Connor, Skip Wilson), I say "thanks."

While in the NBA, I was proud to be the assistant for Paul Westhead, Jim Lynam, Don Chaney, Gene Shue, Chris Ford, and John Calipari. As a head coach my gratitude to Dave Twardzik, Jim Eyen, Bob Staak, Joe Smith, Eddie Jordan, Mike O'Koren, and again, Jim Lynam.

Lute Olson, Hubie Brown, Dean Smith, Sonny Allen, C. Allan Rowe, Jim Dutcher, Jack McKinney, Dick Harter, Rick Majerus, Digger Phelps, Bob Weinhauer, Vic Bubas, and Bucky Walters all allowed me to call, ask questions, and attend practices for further knowledge. This was an amazing experience for a young coach. Additional thanks to these coaches as well:

Jack McCloskey, who exposed the "Penn State Zone" to Philadelphia, also allowed me on-site viewing and answered my questions.

Harry Litwack, "The Chief," who also had an open door policy for practices, made me privy to his match-up zone principles. This mentorship eventually led to my becoming his first full-time assistant at Temple and eventually succeeding him there following his retirement.

Jack Ramsay, an aggressive coach on both ends was the press guru of his day. The 3-1-1 was one of terror, and he taught all who wanted to learn, along with his unique zone offensive set.

During what became the most difficult time of my coaching career, several individuals provided me with a level of support that to this day I am most grateful for:

Bob Knight I first met in 1964, while he was recruiting Jim Oxley, one of my high school players. "Ox" went on to West Point and teamed with Coach K for a formidable back court. As a friend and fellow coach, his advice and public statements stemmed the negative tide swelling against me.

Wayne Hardin is a coach's coach, a brilliant offensive tactician at the Naval Academy (Navy) and Temple. Wayne was a confidant and advisor. He helped guide me through that difficult period and is a good man for all.

Ernie Casale and **Jim Shea** both stuck by me through tough times as well. Rob Ades, a friend, confident, and family lawyer has been there from Temple through the present—a real "mensch." And thanks to **Frank Dolson** and **Dick Weiss**, who, as lead writers for the *Philadelphia Inquirer* and *Daily News* exposed—and put a halt to as a result—what many saw as the undermining of a sound basketball program.

That program was of course Temple's, and following my leaving in 1971 a group of players unjustly not found in the Temple Hall of Fame still deserves the recognition that their hard work, determined play, and performance while representing the University should have earned them. Among them are **Marty Stahurski**, the 13th leading scorer in Temple's history and All Big 5 1st Team from 1976–77 and 1978–79, and **Rick Reed**, who during the 1978–79 season had 208 assists and was named All Big 5 and Big 5 MVP. In addition **Alton McCullough** (1979–1982—Temple's 39th all-time leading scorer), **Keith Parham** (1979–1981—Temple's 35th all-time leading scorer), and **Walt Montford** (1975–1979—Temple's 36th all-time leading scorer). These fine players have been denied the opportunity to say to their children and grandchildren "I'm in the Temple Hall of Fame," but they're hall of famers in my book, and I hope someday the powers-that-be do the right thing and acknowledge them accordingly.

Finally, players win games; they are the most important component of any coaches' success. My gratitude to the high school teams that responded to the zone slides. They practiced, worked hard, and won, and were the "pathfinders" for Bishop Eustace Preparatory School. Temple players were more of the same, and did the best they could within the realms of their set schedules and facilities—I thank you all.

Coauthor Casey also would like to offer special notes of appreciation to the following individuals for their role in the development of Own the Zone.

David Stern—for all he has done for basketball around the world. The NBA is accepted everywhere, and his endorsement of this book was most significant and appreciated.

Michael Goldberg (NABC)—for putting this together, providing encouragement, and stating "this will be good for you." He was right! Thanks, Michael.

Ralph Pim—this book would never have gone to print without him.

Hubie Brown—one of the best minds in the game.

Mark Weinstein—who first brought McGraw-Hill to the table.

Ron Martirano—who succeeded Mark as editor. Thanks to Ron for his patience, persistence, and much needed direction—he tied it all together.

Tom Mocogni—for his time and effort in setting up the photo shoot at Notre Dame College Prep Niles, Illinois. Tom's passion for the game and his players is unmatched.

Major Derrick Stanton, United States Military Academy—who created the diagrams that grace the pages of this book; they are of the highest professional quality. His superb work, done at West Point, is invaluable to this book and the understanding its creators hope to impart.

Rena Copperman and Bob Tinnon—for their outstanding work in the editing and the interior design and layout of this book. It has been a pleasure working together.

Colleen and Bill Schober for their photography and warm hospitality during my visit to Notre Dame College Prep.

The following players and coaches at Notre Dame College Prep who participated in the photo shoot: **Bob Flood, Joe Springer, Eric Hennessey, Kevin Seyter, Rick Szukala, Mike DiGregorio, Marc Bianchini, Mudiaga Eruteya, Andrew Jahns, Nick Lazzara, Matt Weel,** Coach **Luke Yanule,** Coach **Dennis Zelasko,** and Coach **Mike Hennessey**. A special thanks to Father **John Smith**.

And thanks to **Mike Broeker**, deputy athletic director at Marquette University, for providing the outstanding action photos that appear in the book.

Key to Diagrams

Offensive player	1, 2, 3, 4, 5
Offensive player with the ball	①
Defensive player	X_1, X_2, X_3, X_4, X_5
Pass (and direction)	----------▶
Dribble	∿∿∿▶
Screen or pick	———┤
Player movement	———▶
"V" cut	⟍⟋▸

1

Own the Zone

The Basketball System of the Twenty-First Century

In today's fast-changing basketball landscape, coaches must awaken to the fact that there are scores of new challenges, and many traditional theories are no longer true. To be successful in the twenty-first century, coaches must search for innovative strategies that can expand the core tenets of their basketball philosophy.

Own the Zone unlocks the secrets of the zone both defensively and offensively and offers a mint of practical, time-tested information for today's coaches. Defensively, coaches will learn an assortment of strategies that can stop any offensive threat—from a three-point sharpshooter to a penetrating dribbler, from a ball-screening offense to a powerful inside attack. Coaches will become skilled at camouflaging the vulnerable spots in their zone defense so that opponents become confused and hesitant. Defenders will be taught how to play defense one or two passes ahead of the offensive attack. The end result will be a cohesive defensive unit that has the ability to defeat teams with superior size and athleticism.

Offensively, coaches will learn the key principles in zone offense. Players will become proficient at attacking zones and creating high percentage shots against every type of zone defense used in basketball today. Using the zone-busting sets in this book practically guarantees that coaches will never have to worry about playing against zone defenses again.

To survive the perilous coaching profession, coaches must generate opportunities for their teams to win every game. By following the offensive and defensive principles in *Own the Zone*, the authors believe that a team can win 75 percent or more of its games and defeat many of the best opponents on its schedule. Players and coaches will learn how to control the tempo of the game, neutralize an opponent's talent, reduce the number of team fouls, keep their best players on the court, and destroy any zone defense.

Basketball Truths

Many things in basketball are open for debate, but with enough evidence, some issues are indisputable. The first step in *Own the Zone* is to identify seven truths regarding zone defenses. These truths are the bedrock principles for establishing a zone defensive philosophy built on facts rather than on myths.

Truth #1: The Best Way to Upset an Opponent Is to Use a Zone Defense

Many teams are out-talented at three or four positions every time they take the court. To win the battle of the scoreboard, these teams must find a way to neutralize talent. The prescription for beating superior teams consists of four key principles:

1. Control the tempo of the game.
2. Allow your opponent only one shot at the basket.
3. Keep your opponent off the free throw line.
4. Keep your best players out of foul problems.

More often than not, the best way to accomplish all four of these principles and upset a powerful opponent is by using a zone defense. Proof of this statement can be verified by studying the strategies used by international teams that have defeated USA Men's Basketball teams since 2002.

Even though most experts believed that the United States had the most athletic players in the world, the Americans finished sixth in the 2002 World Championships, were embarrassed on the Olympic stage in 2004, and were schooled by Greece, a team that had no National Basketball Association (NBA) players on its roster, in the semifinals of the 2006 World Championships. One of the main reasons for these devastating losses was the inability of Team USA to attack a zone defense. Players repeatedly stood on the perimeter and over-passed without gaining an advantage. The end result was often a three-point attempt as the shot clock was winding down, or a forced shot by a player who penetrated too far into the zone and was double-teamed. The zone defense controlled the tempo of the game and neutralized the athleticism of Team USA.

Author Alexander Wolff credits zone defenses for slowing down the pace and effectiveness of today's star players. "A zone applies brake pads to a game's wheels," explained Wolff. "It forces offenses to put their guards up, literally and figuratively. Played well, particularly in combination with full-court pressure, a zone can pare an offense's 35-second possession down to perhaps 20 workable seconds. Without sound backcourt decision-making, few college teams can be consistently productive in that amount of time."

Historically, many of the greatest upsets in basketball have occurred because of zone defenses. One unforgettable upset took place in the 1983 National Collegiate Athletic Association (NCAA) Finals when

North Carolina State shocked the University of Houston. Entering the tournament with a 25-game winning streak, Houston was ranked number one in both polls. A Houston sportswriter hailed the Cougars, led by 7-foot-tall center Akeem Olajuwon and Clyde Drexler, "Phi Slamma Jamma" because they could leap and dunk like no team before.

Houston's opponent in the semifinals was the second-ranked Louisville Cardinals. Everyone assumed that the victor of this game would easily defeat the winner between North Carolina State and the University of Georgia in the championship match. "Everybody is saying Houston versus Louisville is the heavyweight game and we're the JV [junior varsity] game," said North Carolina State coach Jim Valvano, whose team was trying to become the first NCAA national champion with a double-digit loss total.

North Carolina State slipped by Georgia in the semifinals and was faced with the daunting task of stopping Houston's high-powered offense. The Wolfpack's strategy was to protect the basket area with a packed-in zone defense and play a controlled, slow-down offense. North Carolina State's tactics gave the Wolfpack a five-point lead at halftime. Guy Lewis's Houston team made only 31 percent of their shots and didn't get their first dunk until there were five minutes left.

In the second half, the reenergized Cougars raced to a 42–35 lead. At this point, Lewis ordered his team to go into a spread, stall-like offense to force North Carolina State out of its zone. This maneuver disturbed some of the Houston players. "I felt we should have kept playing the way we were playing," said Larry Micheaux. "Our game is to get up and down the floor and dunk the ball."

North Carolina State edged back and tied the game with two minutes remaining. After a Houston player missed the front end of a one-and-one with 52 seconds remaining, Valvano had the Wolfpack hold the ball for a final shot. In the game's final seconds, North Carolina State attempted a 30-foot desperation shot. The ball was short of the rim, but Lorenzo Charles leaped up and slam-dunked the errant shot with one second remaining. The Wolfpack had miraculously upset Houston 54–52 and limited the Cougars to one slam dunk. It was truly a case of David slaying Goliath, and it would never have occurred if North Carolina State tried to stop Houston in a man-to-man defense.

Truth #2: The Best Strategy to Contain a Superstar Is to Use a Zone Defense

The key to containing a superstar is to limit the number of opportunities that the star player has to exploit the defense. This can be accomplished through strategies such as ball denial and double-teaming. Analyst Dick Vitale applauded the implementation of the zone defense in the NBA because it provided the opportunity to double-team superstars even when they didn't have the ball.

The possibilities are endless for creative-thinking coaches. Some of basketball's best players such as Wilt Chamberlain, Kareem Abdul-Jabbar, and Elvin Hayes have been reduced to a fraction of their greatness by a zone defense.

Chamberlain averaged almost 30 points per game in 1957 and led the University of Kansas into the NCAA finals against the University of North Carolina. In arguably the best college basketball game ever played, North Carolina stunned Kansas 54–53 in triple overtime. Prior to the game, Hall of Fame coach Frank McGuire told his team, "We're not playing Kansas tonight. We're playing Chamberlain. Kansas can't beat you, but Chamberlain can."

McGuire crafted a collapsing zone defense that fronted Chamberlain and triple-teamed him every time he caught the ball. On a shot attempt, McGuire instructed two players to be in front of Chamberlain and two players to squeeze in behind him. The player farthest from Chamberlain was to chase the rebound. Wilt did not score his first basket until there were fewer than five minutes remaining in the first half. Chamberlain was limited to 13 shots and made only six field goals in the loss to the Tar Heels.

UCLA's Lew Alcindor (later Kareem Abdul-Jabbar) and Houston's Elvin Hayes met twice during the 1968 season and both games were decided by a zone defense that stopped the opponent's superstar. During the regular season, the teams played in the Houston Astrodome before 52,693 fans. The number-one-ranked UCLA entered the game with a 47-game winning streak and appeared to be unbeatable, but the second-ranked Cougars were not to be denied. Their 1-3-1 zone defense stifled Alcindor, limiting him to four baskets in 18 attempts. This was the poorest shooting percentage that Alcindor had during his 88-game UCLA career. In Alcindor's defense, he played with an eye injury that handicapped his vision. Hayes scored 39 points (29 in the first half) and pulled down 15 rebounds to lead Houston past UCLA 71–69.

The second meeting occurred in the Final Four, but this time it was UCLA that turned the tables on Hayes. At the suggestion of assistant coach Jerry Norman, the Bruins played a diamond-shaped zone. Hall of Fame coach John Wooden instructed one player to shadow Hayes, another player to be at the top of the free throw circle, and two players to be aligned at the wings, and assigned Alcindor to stay near the basket at all times. This defensive alignment frustrated Hayes, and he was practically eliminated from the Houston offense. Hayes finished with only three field goals in 10 attempts and scored just 10 points. UCLA jumped out to a 22-point lead at halftime and never looked back. They held a 44-point lead before mass substitutions held the final score to 101–69. Houston coach Guy Lewis said it was the greatest exhibition of basketball that he had ever seen.

During the 2006 NBA Play-offs, MVP Dwyane Wade was practically unstoppable. He drove to the basket at will and averaged almost 35 points per game in the NBA finals. It is important to remember that the only time during the NBA play-offs that Wade's penetration was contained was when an opponent played a zone defense. With the ability of today's players to dribble-penetrate, the best way to limit one-on-one opportunities and protect defensive players from foul problems is by using a zone defense.

Truth #3: Championships Are Won by Teams Using a Zone Defense

The old adage that "championship teams do not use a zone defense" is a myth. Ever since the invention of basketball by Dr. James Naismith in 1891, many of the game's most prominent coaches have endorsed the theory that championship teams play man-to-man defense. Through the years, zone defenses have been treated as if they were inferior. It was believed that any team that played a zone defense was admitting they didn't have the talent or the toughness to play man-to-man. Nothing could be further from the truth. "The notion that you're not a man's man if you play a zone is ridiculous," said Tom Izzo, head coach of Michigan State. "Sometimes we let our egos get in the way of our brains."

A quick history lesson will confirm that zone defenses do win championships. In fact, zone defenses were significant factors in determining the championship teams in the first National Invitational Tournament (NIT) in 1938 and the NCAA tournament in 1939.

In the inaugural NIT championship game, Temple University utilized a 3-2 zone defense, designed by assistant coach Harry Litwack, and walloped Colorado 60–36. A sportswriter from the *New York Times* described the action in these words: "Colorado was helpless. . . . Temple's zone defense was a rock barrier and clamped down on the Colorado shooters like a net."

A year later, Oregon's 3-2 zone defense throttled Ohio State's high-powered offense to win the first NCAA championship. Unlike most teams in 1939, Oregon did not rely solely upon either a man-to-man or zone defense. Their astute young coach, Howard Hobson, used multiple defenses. Based on his highly accurate scouting report, Hobson started the championship game in a zone defense to offset Ohio State's explosive offense. The Buckeyes were disjointed and out-of-synch as Hobson's team alternated between a zone defense and man-to-man defense. The end result was a commanding 13-point victory.

In 1979, Michigan State's 2-3 match-up zone stifled Larry Bird and his Indiana State teammates, and the Spartans won the national title 75–64. The game captured the fancy of basketball fans everywhere as it pitted Larry Bird, the leader of the number-one-ranked and undefeated Sycamores, against Michigan State's magic man, Earvin Johnson.

Bill Hodges, Indiana State's first-year coach, knew the key to beating Michigan State was securing a lead substantial enough to pull the Spartans out of its patented 2-3 zone, but that never occurred. Indiana State led just three times the entire game, all in the first five minutes.

Bird, who had scored 35 points and converted on 16 of 19 field-goal attempts in the semifinal game against DePaul, made only seven field goals in 21 attempts. Coaching legend Jud Heathcote made a slight coaching adjustment in his 2-3 zone that proved to be the difference in the victory over Indiana State. "We had one man and a half on Bird whenever he put the ball on the floor," said Heathcote. "We had a forward on him and a guard came in to help. It was a gamble because Bird is such a team player, but it paid off for us."

Fast-forward to the year 2006. That was when the zone defense was a determining factor in Spain's world championship in the Federal International Basketball Association (FIBA) and the Miami Heat's championship in the NBA. Pepu Hernández, the Spain's brilliant coach, led his team to their first-ever world title by continually switching between zone and man-to-man defenses. Their dominating 23-point victory over Greece in the championship game was the greatest team sporting achievement in Spain's history.

In the NBA play-offs, Pat Riley led the Miami Heat to the championship by masterfully alternating his defenses and controlling the tempo of the game. As a young coach, Riley was christened into a basketball world in which man-to-man defense was the "right way" to play. Riley's hard-nosed, tenacious defense was demonstrated in Los Angeles, New York, and Miami. "When you study the legendary teams in basketball, you will discover that all those teams combined talent with great defense," Riley said. "You've got to stop other teams to win."

Through the years, Riley has convinced his players that showy dunks make the highlight films, but a devotion to defense wins championships. Heat center Alonzo Mourning said, "Riley has drilled defense into us so much in practices that it's become instinctual."

When the NBA approved the use of a restricted zone defense (a defender cannot stay in the lane more than three seconds) in 2001, most basketball experts agreed they would never see a Riley-coached team playing a zone. Initially they were right, but in typical Riley fashion, he pulled off a coaching gem in the 2006 NBA Finals. He employed zone defenses at strategic points in the series to change the pace of the game. Dallas was taken out of their offensive flow, and the momentum shifted to Miami's advantage. After losing the first two games, the Heat stormed back and won four straight games to claim the NBA title.

Truth #4: An Opponent's Zone Offense Is Not as Good as Its Man-to-Man Offense

Most coaches spend the majority of their practice time working against a man-to-man defense. As a result, their team's zone offense is not nearly as good. Successful coaches formulate their game plans on the theory that the more an opponent must utilize their weakest offense, the less chance they have for victory.

Bill Self, head coach at Kansas, thinks that a zone defense can take a team out of its rhythm and create a psychological disadvantage for the offense. "Some teams, including us, just don't attack the zone very well," said Self. "We have a tendency to stand around. Sometimes, when zones go up as a change of pace, teams don't attack it well for two or three possessions, and players think, 'this is a great zone' and it gets mental."

Tom Izzo believes one of the reasons Michigan State has been successful with their zone defense is because many teams do not work on zone offense every day in practice, and their players are not well schooled in the best ways to beat a zone.

It is the same story in the NBA. Coaches at the highest level have been slow to embrace the zone defense, but they have been even slower in their development of a zone offense. Very little practice time is spent working on zone offense. Consequently, even an average zone defense will be successful against most teams.

Longtime NBA coach George Karl hasn't seen a lot of inventiveness when it comes to zone offense. "When I see a zone, I see only four or five different zone offenses," Karl said. "There's not a lot of creativity to it as compared to a man-to-man offense."

Because a team's zone offense is normally weaker than its man-to-man offense, periodically switching defenses is an excellent strategy because it keeps opponents off-balance and reduces the number of possessions that you have to defend against a team's best plays.

Truth #5: The Pick-and-Roll Is Best Defended with a Zone Defense

The toughest play to defend in basketball has always been the pick-and-roll, and the best way to defend it is with a zone defense. Over the past decade, there has been a resurgence of the pick-and-roll in college and high school basketball. During the 1970s and 1980s, most teams used the passing game (also called the motion offense), which discouraged setting screens for the ball handler. As a result, teams from that era did not have to defend against the pick-and-roll like teams do today.

The defensive demise of the USA Men's Team in the 2006 World Championship Semifinals was its inability to stop the high pick-and-roll. After the game, ESPN Basketball analyst Jay Bilas said, "The screen-and-roll is difficult to defend. It always has been, and when run right, always will be. Greece did a great job of keeping the floor spread, taking the defender down to the line of the screen, and making the right reads off of it. Most importantly, Greece hit shots. The Greeks scored 101 points in just 40 minutes."

After his team's loss, Dwyane Wade said, "We had such a difficult time stopping their screen-and-roll. I wished we had changed up and showed them a little zone." Wade was not being critical of his coaches. He was just stating the fact there is a specific time and place for a zone defense.

One definite place for the zone is against teams that set a lot of screens for the ball handler. A zone defense minimizes the effectiveness of this maneuver because it places the defenders in help positions. With the emphasis on ball vision, zone defensive players can anticipate and defend against ball screens.

Truth #6: A Zone Defense Complements a Fast-Break Offense

It is a myth that teams cannot rebound effectively out of a zone defense. For decades, coaches have preached that a zone defense results in poor rebounding because the defenders do not have assigned opponents to block out. In reality, every defender still has the responsibility of blocking out an opponent. The advantage of playing a zone defense is that the players are positioned in prime rebounding areas.

A zone defense is a perfect complement to fast-break basketball. Hall of Fame coach Eddie Hickey changed the complexion of the game by designing the three-lane fast break during the 1940s. The catalyst for Hickey's much-celebrated fast break was his zone defense. Hickey's inside defenders were trained to block out, get the missed shot, and make a quick outlet pass. Hall of Fame player "Easy" Ed Macauley said, "As soon as I rebounded the ball, my teammates took off and I passed to a player at the wing. One man brought the ball up in the middle of the floor, and there was a player on either side of him racing down the court. Our fast break was built on speed. We had to be fast and pass the ball ahead to open teammates."

A zone defense has helped Paul Westhead, nicknamed the "Guru of Go," develop a fast-break system second-to-none. Relentless rebounding and quick outlet passing spearheads Westhead's high-powered offense, and he believes these are best accomplished using a zone defense. At Loyola Marymount, the Lions raced to the Elite Eight in the 1990 NCAA Tournament averaging 122 points per game, which still stands as an NCAA record.

Truth #7: A Zone Defense Encourages Team Play

Zone defenses are built on teamwork and communication. Players learn how to play together and discover that basketball success depends on having a five-person team on the court every second of the game. Teaching players how to play the zone defense addresses one of the biggest problems in today's game—the lack of team play.

Most basketball experts claim there has been a significant decline in team play in men's basketball over the past 10 years on all levels of competition. International basketball expert Fran Fraschilla thinks the decline in international basketball success for the United States is not a question of raw talent. He believes the underlying issue is the evolution over the past couple of decades to a "me-first, highlights-driven style of play" in the United States. "It has compromised our ability to play team basketball," said Fraschilla, "which is really impacting the quality of the game in the U.S."

Today's young players are growing up in a culture that promotes individual stars. Players and fans celebrate spectacular individual performances and often miss the beauty of five players working together. Many rising stars in the millennial generation are choosing style over substance, and the beauty of teamwork is slowly vanishing from the playgrounds and gymnasiums across our nation.

Teaching players the correct way to play a zone defense is an excellent technique to build team play. Players learn how to communicate and move together as a single unit. They discover the power of teamwork because defense cannot be played properly with fewer than five players working together. In time, they will develop a sense of pride in knowing that they can stop any offensive threat.

On the flip side, learning how to attack a zone defense teaches teamwork and solidarity of purpose. Each player discovers that, individually, he or she cannot beat a zone defense. Players must learn proper spacing, ball reversal, inside-outside action, and dribble penetration to force the defense to collapse in order to free a teammate for an open shot. Donnie Nelson, the director of player personnel for the Dallas Mavericks, applauded the introduction of the zone into the NBA because he believed, in the long run, it would be good for the game of basketball in the United States. "If the NBA is encouraging our guys to shoot and pass, then our young kids watching NBA basketball will grow up wanting to do the same things."

Changing a Mind-Set

The stigma of a zone defense is so ingrained in today's culture that many coaches and players still believe that playing a zone is not a manly thing. Rasheed Wallace of the Detroit Pistons is one of the most vociferous adversaries of the zone defense. Prior to the 2007 season, Wallace said, "Zone is a get-by defense. To me, man-to-man instills pride. But in that zone, you can blame other people. You can say, 'Oh you didn't get to that spot. I was out here, but you weren't over there.' With the man defense, there ain't nobody to blame but yourself."

NBA head coach Flip Saunders recognizes the reluctance of most NBA players to play zone. "For some reason, whenever you say *zone* it's like those are the worst four letters in the NBA," Saunders said. "Players hear *zone*, and they get nervous. But it's not about being macho. You know what macho is? Macho is about winning. In this game you have to utilize what you have. If you have a team with a lot of length and quickness like we have, it's an advantage to play zone. And doing that will make our man defense better."

"I've heard a lot of college coaches say they don't like playing zones," said Indiana coach Kelvin Sampson. "Well, a coach likes to win, and if it takes a zone to win, he'll like it fine."

Legendary coach Eddie Sutton believes the biggest reason that today's players do not like zones is that they can't consistently beat them. "Against a zone, a star player tends to stymie himself," Sutton said. "He doesn't move, doesn't pass, and therefore doesn't score."

In reality, the pros and cons of the zone defense will be debated as long as the game is played. There will always be coaches who oppose the zone and will spend very little time teaching zone concepts both offensively and defensively. These are the same coaches who will be the easiest to beat because their players will not be prepared to defeat a zone defense.

The first step to success is to have an open mind and an eagerness to learn. *Own the Zone* provides the opportunity for coaches to expand their knowledge and design strategies that will overpower their opponents.

2

The Evolution of the Zone Defense and Zone Press

Throughout the history of basketball, most defenses were created out of necessity. The constant improvement of individual skills and team offenses forced coaches to experiment with different defensive alignments and strategies. Even the rules favored the offensive team, so it has been a continuous battle for coaches to try and keep the offense from getting too far ahead.

This chapter provides a condensed history of the zone defense and zone press to preserve the legacies of many coaching legends and spark the creativity of today's coaches so they can discover defensive strategies to stop today's offensive players. Studying the evolution of the zone defense and zone press will provide an indispensable framework for appreciating the beliefs that defined a particular era, and more importantly, it will help build a springboard for futuristic thinking.

In the Beginning

The only type of defense used during basketball's first 20 years was a full-court man-to-man defense. A player was responsible for one opponent and followed this player all over the court. When a team lost possession of the ball, its players immediately located their assigned opponents and "stuck with them like glue" until the ball was recovered. The game's founder, Dr. James Naismith, instructed defensive players to do everything within the rules to prevent their opponents from getting the ball. This style of defense required a tremendous amount of stamina and energy.

The Line Defense

A new type of defense evolved around 1910 called the "line defense." Instead of following opponents all over the backcourt, defenders retreated to the middle of the floor and formed a line that stretched from one sideline to the other. It developed in professional basketball because coaches and players began to realize the importance of protecting the area closest to the basket.

The line defense resembled the goal-line stand in football. It was designed to stop any player with the ball from getting through. Each defender in the line either guarded the closest opponent to his or her designated starting spot, much like today's match-up zone, or had a preassigned opponent to defend and picked up that player at the midcourt area.

Walter "Doc" Meanwell, one of the most influential coaches during the early days of basketball, designed a five-man two-line defense. He created this defense because it was becoming more and more difficult for one defender to stop a talented offensive player. In practice it was still a man-to-man defense, but it was the catalyst for future zones and marked the birth of team defense. Meanwell's ingenuity helped the University of Wisconsin win national championships in 1912, 1914, and 1916, and earned him a spot in the inaugural class enshrined in the Naismith Memorial Basketball Hall of Fame in Springfield, Massachusetts.

In Meanwell's five-man two-line defense, the center (X_5) and two forwards $(X_3$ and $X_4)$ retreated to the middle of the court and created the first line of defense. The guards $(X_1$ and $X_2)$ formed the second line of defense approximately 12 feet behind the front line.

The first two offensive players down the court were permitted to run past the front line of defense. As shown in Diagram 2.1, the two defenders in the second line $(X_1$ and $X_2)$ were responsible for these offensive players and guarded them using man-to-man principles. After two opponents passed the front line, no offensive player was allowed to go past without being defended.

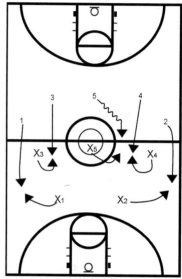

Diagram 2.1 Two-Line Defensive Coverage

The First Zone Defense

The zone defense was invented in 1914 in a game played between Bristol (West Virginia) High School and the Grafton YMCA. The novel defense was created as a remedy for a slippery playing surface caused by a leaky roof. During the first half, the court became so slick that players spent much of the time slipping and sliding. Future Hall of Fame coach Clair Bee was a player on the Grafton YMCA team. "I remember the game distinctly," said Bee. "It was the first time in my life that I ever played with older fellows. The reason that I played was the floor was so slippery in the first half, and I was the only one who could stand up."

At halftime Cam Henderson, coach of the Bristol team, designed a strategy that became the first zone defense. "I told the boys there was no point running after those boys from Grafton, when they got the ball," said Henderson. "We'd just stand still. I went out there and showed them how to line up. There were three boys out front and two back. It worked out just fine on that wet court."

Cam Henderson: The Architect of the Zone Defense

Cam Henderson was fascinated with the potential of his new defense, and it became a mainstay during his illustrious coaching career at Bristol High School, Muskingum College, Davis & Elkins College, and Marshall University. Henderson's innovative mind revolutionized the game by combining the zone with a fast break. He portrayed the zone defense and fast break as twins, with the zone being born first, followed by the fast break. Clair Bee said that Henderson's 1938 squad was the best that he had ever seen in transition from a zone defense to a fast-break offense.

The original zone used by Henderson was a 3-2, but he soon discovered that it did not provide the necessary rebounding to support his fast-break offense. Cam's solution was to drop one of the front defenders back, creating a 2-3 alignment. Henderson positioned the team's best dribbler on the front line and assigned him to be the middleman on the fast break. The other front-line defender filled the outside lane on the right side.

Henderson demanded that the players filling the outside lanes sprint to the basket. In the early gymnasiums, the baskets were mounted on the walls at the end of the court, and most facilities did not even have pads attached to the walls. The safest thing for a player to do was to slow down so that he did not run into the wall. But with the determination that Henderson required of his teams, this option was not acceptable. Henderson's players pursued the basket without regard to their own personal safety, which often resulted in a two-on-one or a three-on-two situation.

There were many unforgettable games during Henderson's illustrious career. One of them occurred in 1938 when Marshall upset Long Island University and snapped the Blackbirds 40-game winning streak. Another took place in 1947 when Henderson led Marshall to the National Association of Intercollegiate Athletics (NAIA) national championship with his zone defense and fast-break offense.

The Rise in Zone Defenses

The zone defensive concept of guarding a designated area rather than a specific player spread quickly during the 1920s. In the zone, a specific area defined the responsibility of each player, and his vision was primarily on the ball rather than an assigned opponent. Three key factors in the rise in popularity of the zone defense were: (1) continuity offenses, (2) poor perimeter shooting, and (3) small gymnasiums.

Continuity Offenses

During basketball's early era, there were no set offensive formations or plays. The game was helter-skelter with one player, usually a forward, attempting most of the shots. The guards were the defenders and rarely ventured from the defensive end of the court, while the center was the intermediary between the forwards and the guards.

Things quickly changed during the 1910s and 1920s when innovative coaches such as Doc Meanwell and H. C. "Doc" Carlson choreographed offenses that highlighted precise patterns and sharp passing for the purpose of getting an uncontested layup shot. Meanwell called his system "scientific basketball." In his first three years at Wisconsin, he led the Badgers to a 44–1 record and two national championships. Meanwell's offense captured the attention of the basketball world, and coaches from the East Coast to the West Coast began emulating his methods.

Basketball historians credit Carlson with creating the first true continuity offense. It was called the "figure 8 offense" and had three players moving and two players stationary. Carlson later developed a four-player and a five-player continuity. He also used two types of continuity—one including the dribble and the other excluding it. During a 12-year period, Pittsburgh won 80 percent of their games using Carlson's continuity offense. Joe Lapchick, the legendary Hall of Fame coach from St. John's University, claimed that every modern offensive scheme evolved from the innovations of Carlson.

The continuity offense featured set patterns that would be run over and over again until a player was open for a high percentage shot. This methodical and disciplined style of play was so successful that many teams opted to play a zone defense so they would not have to defend against the constant cutting and screening of the offensive players. It is interesting to note that Doc Carlson at Pittsburgh compiled only a 50 percent winning record after opponents started defending his figure 8 offense with a zone defense.

Poor Perimeter Shooting

The second reason for the increase of zone defenses was the lack of proficient perimeter shooters. During the early years of basketball, the skill of shooting a ball through a hoop was practically nonexistent. A team was fortunate if it had one good shooter on its squad.

Clair Bee described the roles of the players in this era in these words: "One of the guards was known as the 'standing guard'—he stood; the other was the 'running guard'—he ran; the 'center' jumped; the 'feeding forward' fed; the 'shooting forward' made all the baskets, shot all the fouls, was captain of the team, was president of the class, married the banker's daughter, became governor, always believed he should have been president, and, what was more tragic, got all the write-ups." In addition to highlighting Bee's colorful personality, this description also illustrates that there were very few good shooters during this period of basketball.

Supporters of the zone believed it was advantageous for the defense to be located closer to the basket so the defenders would be in position to stop layup shots and be able to rebound any missed attempts. They also theorized that because the ball could be in only one designated zone area at a time, there would always be a defender present to challenge a shooter.

Small Gymnasiums

The third reason for the increase in popularity of the zone defense was the size of the gymnasiums where the majority of high schools and colleges played their games. It was not uncommon to compete on courts that were only 60 feet long and 40 feet wide. Many of these gymnasiums had low ceilings, which made outside shooting almost prohibitive. In facilities such as these, it was best to position your defenders under the basket in a zone defense.

Many gymnasiums had balconies with running tracks above the courts. The balconies often protruded over the court, which made it impossible to shoot from the dead corner. Innovative coaches created specialized zone defenses for gymnasiums such as these.

Basketball's Civil War

During the first 50 years of basketball, the zone defense created a conflict between coaches who wanted the zone banned and those who believed the zone was good for the game. It caused sit-down strikes by offensive players, booing and heckling by spectators, and feuds between coaches, players, and fans.

Legendary coaches Doc Meanwell and Clair Bee believed zone defenses had an important place in the game. Meanwell thought the zone was the best method to stop a talented offensive scorer. Bee, regarded as one of the game's greatest strategists, said, "The intelligent coach recognizes the strength and weakness of each defense and impartially adapts either, both, or a variation, to the material available. Players who denounce the zone in basketball are usually unfamiliar with its use and methods of attacking it."

On the other side of the argument were multitudes of coaches who thought zone defenses were ruining basketball. They were concerned that zones would cause a serious decrease of interest in the game. Dr. Naismith opposed the zone defense because "it tends to stall a game that was devised to be constantly on the attack."

In certain regions of the country, adversaries of the zone defense made a "gentleman's agreement" that zones would not be employed. Others coaches tried to create rules that would outlaw the use of zone defenses. Forrest "Phog" Allen, called the "Father of Basketball Coaching," recommended enlarging the width of the playing court to 80 feet, which would make it almost impossible for a team to use a zone defense. Allen believed the only time to use zone tactics occurred when a defensive team was outnumbered on a fast break. In situations such as the three-on-two, Allen instructed his defenders to form a tandem. Their top priority was to prevent a layup. Allen, known for his oratory brilliance, called this type of defense the "stratified transitional man-to-man defense with zone principles."

H.C. "Doc" Carlson, who led Pittsburgh to national championships in 1928 and 1930, despised zones and thought they disrupted the action of the game. He called the zone "tactless" and believed the best way to show people the ridiculousness of the zone defense was to hold the ball and not even attempt to score. Basketball at that time did not have the 10-second rule, so Carlson's players would often use a stall and never cross midcourt. Against archrival Penn State's zone defense, the Pittsburgh players stayed at their end of the court, dribbling, passing, sitting on the ball, and even playing cards.

Hall of Fame coach Frank Keaney described the zone defense as "un-American." He used tactics similar to Carlson's to display his hatred of zone defenses. Angry that the University of Maine went into a zone in an attempt to keep the score close, Keaney called time out and instructed his Rhode Island players to go into a deep freeze until Maine came out of their zone. The Black Bears of Maine refused to budge. With a 4–0 lead, a Rhode Island player stood with the ball under his arm practically the entire first half. Other players sat on the floor, while the substitutes read newspapers. As Keaney left the floor he shouted, "If you really want to play a zone, we'll help you."

Future Hall of Fame coaches Nat Holman (City College at New York) and Branch McCracken (Indiana University) advocated the use of a man-to-man defense and discouraged young coaches from using zones. In 1935, Holman said, "I have never seen or heard of a team of any consequence that employed a zone defense. I strongly advise against its general use." (It should be mentioned that Holman, the only coach to ever win the NCAA and NIT tournaments in the same season, changed his stance on the zone defense later in his career and recognized its merits against certain types of offenses.)

McCracken said, "It has always been my belief that if every coach used a zone defense we would hurt the game of basketball. Especially if the offensive team gets a few points ahead and works on the theory of spreading the defense by holding the ball out and making the zone come after it."

Between 1929 and 1931, the St. John's basketball team, nicknamed the "The Wonder Five" won 68 out of 72 games. Their strategies included stalling on offense, holding the ball at the far end of the court, and cleverly passing the ball back and forth until there was an uncontested layup shot. As more and more teams utilized full court stalling tactics, zone defenses lost some of their popularity during the late 1920s.

Rule Changes

Three rule changes resulted in a resurgence of zone defenses. In 1933, in spite of Dr. Naismith's strong disapproval, basketball adopted the 10-second rule. This rule forced the offensive team to advance the ball across the center-court line within 10 seconds. The full-court stalling tactics used by dominating teams such as Pittsburgh and St. John's were no longer possible with the 10-second rule.

The second rule change that encouraged zone defense enthusiasts was the three-second rule. This rule, adopted in 1936, placed a three-second restriction on an offensive player in the free throw lane area and eliminated the most powerful strategic weapon of the offense. No longer could teams permanently position their pivot player under the basket during their offensive attack.

The widening of the free throw lane from six feet to 12 feet in 1956 also increased the popularity of zone defenses. Many coaches felt that the wider lane, coupled with the three-second rule, strengthened zone defenses to the point that it would be foolish for coaches not to use them.

Even then, some coaches stayed true to their belief that zones were bad for the sport. Norm Sloan, who led North Carolina State to the NCAA national championship in 1974, said, "I hate the zone defense. It looks like a stick-up at the 7-Eleven. Five guys standing there with their hands in the air."

Regarding rule changes and the popularity of the zone defense, the game of basketball is at an interesting junction with the passing of the legislation in 2007 that extends the three-point line in men's basketball by one foot. Many basketball experts predict that there will be a significant increase in the number of zone defenses when the new distance goes into effect during the 2008 season.

3-2 Zone Defense

The most popular zone defense in the 1920s was the 3-2 zone. It was patterned after the five-man two-line defense. The defenders retreated to their assigned area, focused their attention on the ball, and generally remained on a fixed spot on the floor. One of the advantages of the 3-2 zone was that it created fast-break opportunities due to the lack of defensive balance by opponents.

The 3-2 provided strong coverage against perimeter shooters, but as discussed, it did not always provide strong rebounding. Many times the two inside defenders were out-rebounded because there were more offensive players going after the missed shot. Other weak spots in the 3-2 zone were in the high post area and the corners.

As offensive players became more skilled in passing, shooting, and screening, it became necessary for coaches to modify the stationary 3-2 zone. Innovators such as George Keogan, Eddie Hickey, and Harry Litwack introduced strategies to counter the advances in offensive play.

George Keogan's Shifting Man-to-Man Defense

Notre Dame's George Keogan introduced the technique of switching into his man-to-man defense in an attempt to stop the heralded figure 8 offense used by rival coach Doc Carlson at Pittsburgh. He believed this was the best way to defend against opponents that used two-man screening plays as the foundation for their offense. On every screen, the defensive player being screened shouted, "Shift!" This signaled that both defenders should switch defensive assignments.

Keogan's defense became known as the "shifting man-to-man," although it was really a zone defense. It was so successful that from 1927 to 1931, Notre Dame held their opponents under 30 points in all but five games. Keogan led the Fighting Irish to national championships in 1927 and 1936. His switching technique became the hallmark for outstanding teams in the 1930s and 1940s.

Eddie Hickey's 3-2 Zone Defense

In 1948, St. Louis University won the NIT championship by combining Keogan's switching tactics with a fast-break offense. Coach Eddie Hickey developed a three-lane fast break built on precision passing, ball handling, and rebounding. Hall of Fame coach Pete Newell credits Hickey's fast-break principles as being the foundation for today's fast break.

Hickey's fast break was dependent upon first obtaining possession of the basketball. In 1948, Hickey positioned Ed Macauley and Marv Schatzman in the back line of his 3-2 zone defense to take advantage of their height and rebounding skills. Macauley, a two-time All-American and future NBA All-Star, made quick outlet passes to ignite a blazing fast break.

The defenders on the front line created havoc for poor ball-handling teams by switching on every screen. This created turnovers and additional fast-break opportunities. Hickey was inducted into the

Naismith Memorial Basketball Hall of Fame and was the first coach in basketball history to lead three different universities (Creighton, St. Louis, and Marquette) into the NCAA tournament.

Harry Litwack's 3-2 Zone and Box-and-One Defense

Harry Litwack not only developed one of the best 3-2 zone defenses in the country, but he also introduced the box-and-one defense during his illustrious coaching career at Temple University. The box-and-one defense had four players in a zone defense while one defender player guarded the opponent's star player in a man-to-man defense.

Under Litwack's leadership (freshman coach from 1931–1947; head coach from 1947–1973), the zone defense became the trademark for Temple Basketball. Seventy-five years later, the trademark still exists. Coauthor Casey served as an assistant for Coach Litwack and continued the storied tradition during his tenure as head coach. John Chaney followed suit and made the zone defense a mainstay during his Hall of Fame career at Temple.

Many basketball historians believe that Litwack's zone defense helped him achieve "more success with less," than any other coach in history. Litwack wanted his players to be aggressive, force the action, and keep the ball out of the middle of the floor. He was also one of the first coaches to teach his frontcourt players to stretch their arms to the side rather than over their heads, because it made it tougher for the offense to pass the ball inside.

Between 1956 and 1958, Litwack led Temple to three consecutive third-place finishes in national tournaments behind the nation's dynamic duo of All-American Guy Rodgers and future NBA star Hal Lear. During this period, Litwack mixed his defenses between his patented zone and a man-to-man. Litwack got this idea from watching the Harlem Globetrotters play against the College All-Stars. The Globetrotters constantly switched on all exchanges and cuts to the basket in order to conserve energy due to their enormous playing schedule. Litwack saw how it confused the College All-Stars and decided to incorporate it into his defensive system.

"All we did was tell our star player, Guy Rodgers, that when we yelled 'Going through,' we were in a man-to-man defense and if not, we were to be in a zone defense," said Litwack. Temple finished third in the NCAA tournament in 1956, defeated St. Bonaventure for third place in the NIT in 1957, and lost a heart-breaker to Kentucky in the NCAA semifinals, before they beat Kansas State to capture another third place finish in 1958. During Litwack's 21-year career as head coach, he led the Owls to 13 postseason tournaments, including the 1969 NIT Championship.

2-3 Zone Defense

Cam Henderson designed the 2-3 zone defense to strengthen his team's rebounding so it could get the ball out quicker on the fast break. It also provided stronger coverage of the basket area. The back-line defenders were positioned to keep the ball out of the lane, block out, and rebound. The 2-3 alignment was used effectively against teams that had poor perimeter shooters.

2-1-2 Zone Defense

The 2-1-2 zone defense evolved as a compromise between the 3-2 and the 2-3 zones. The success created by positioning an offensive player in the high post resulted in the 2-1-2 zone defense, which placed a defender near the free throw line. Its rise in popularity was also due to the rule change in 1956, which widened the free throw lane from six feet to 12 feet. The increased size of the free throw lane, along with the three-second rule, moved offensive post players farther away from the basket.

Many coaches, such as Frank McGuire, believed that the 2-1-2 zone was the best alignment to defend both the low post and the high post areas. It also positioned three players in the all-important re-bound triangle. (See Diagram 2.2.) With practice, defenders X_3, X_4,

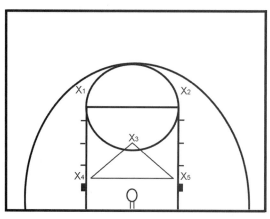

Diagram 2.2 The Rebound Triangle

and X_5 were able to control the boards and practically eliminate scoring in this area. The rebound-triangle concept is still a key component in basketball success today.

1-3-1 Zone Defense

Clair Bee invented the 1-3-1 zone defense in 1937, and it became a favorite for his powerful Long Island University teams. He designed the zone so that his team could place defenders in front and behind an opponent's star pivot player. Bee's theory was to keep three defensive players between the ball and the basket at all times. The three-in-line principle was applied at every opportunity.

Bee employed the 1-3-1 defense almost exclusively during the 1942 season. Only when Long Island was behind and it was late in the game did Bee resort to a man-to-man defense. Bee directed the Blackbirds into the national limelight during the 1930s and 1940s. His Long Island teams recorded two undefeated seasons and won the NIT in 1939 and 1941.

1-2-2 Zone Defense

The 1-2-2 zone defense closely resembled the 3-2 zone. Clair Bee called the 1-2-2 zone the "jug defense." The defensive player defending the ball handler repre- sented the neck of the jug. The next line of defense formed the shoulders of the jug, and the last line of players formed the base of the jug. (See Diagram 2.3.)

As the ball was moved from one part of the floor to another, the position of the defenders changed, but the outline of the jug was maintained. The defensive player guarding the ball always represented the neck of the jug. The four other players arranged themselves so that two formed the shoulders and two formed the base of the jug. Bee thought if the players kept the thought of a jug in mind, the shifts were extremely simple.

Coaches such as Jack McCloskey (Pennsylvania and Wake Forest), Ray Mears (Wittenberg

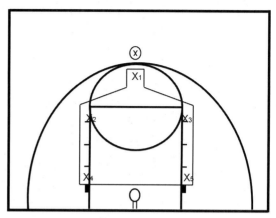

Diagram 2.3 1-2-2 Zone Defense, "The Jug"

and Tennessee), and Eldon Miller (Wittenberg and Ohio State) were recognized for their outstanding 1-2-2 defenses. McCloskey became the head coach at Wake Forest University in 1967 and introduced the 1-2-2 zone defense to the Atlantic Coast Conference. North Carolina's coach Dean Smith claimed that McCloskey's adaptation of the 1-2-2 was the most difficult of the straight zones to attack.

"There was a time when we had some reservations about using the 1-2-2 zone," said Smith.

"We felt that the alignment was lacking in the all-important middle, where the offenses like to have the ball. The credit for changing our minds belongs to Jack McCloskey. They hustled their people in and out of the middle very effectively."

John Lawther's Penn State Sliding Zone Defense

John Lawther became a national expert on a combination defense that he called the "sliding zone defense." It is interesting to note that Lawther became a basketball coach strictly by happenstance. In 1926, Lawther, the head football coach at Westminster College (Pennsylvania), was asked by the college president to fill in as basketball coach for the final two games of the season. Lawther reluctantly agreed. Westminster lost both games, finished the campaign winless, and Lawther quickly turned his attention back to football. But the president of the college came calling again and convinced Lawther to be the permanent coach of both football and basketball. It proved to be the defining moment for basketball at Westminster College.

Lawther realized that his basketball players did not have the talent to defeat most of the opponents on his schedule. He benched seven returning lettermen and introduced the sliding zone defense. Utilizing taller players and a zone defense, Westminster finished with the best season in seven years. During his 10 years as head basketball coach, Lawther's teams won 166 games while losing only 36. His most memorable moment came in 1934 when he guided Westminster to a 37–33 victory over undefeated St. John's in the first college basketball doubleheader at Madison Square Garden.

Lawther then coached Penn State for 13 seasons, and the Nittany Lions became famous for their zone defense, which became known as the "Penn State Sliding Zone." In 1942, he led Penn State to a first-round upset of the University of Illinois, the top-seeded team in the NCAA tournament. When asked by Clair Bee why he used the sliding zone, Lawther replied, "Because you guys haven't learned how to beat it yet."

The basic concepts in Lawther's defense were "playing the ball" and "sliding." The first concept required every defender to see the ball at all times. The second concept necessitated each defenders sliding to a new floor position on any movement of the ball. Lawther's teams often alternated between a 3-2 zone and a 2-3 zone in an attempt to confuse the opposition. After his retirement from coaching, Lawther's sliding zone defense continued to win basketball games through his former players and assistants, Elmer Gross and John Egli.

Gross utilized Lawther's sliding zone after being named head coach at Penn State in 1949. He directed the Nittany Lions to an 80–40 record and two NCAA tournament berths in five years. Gross used primarily a 3-2 alignment. He believed the first step in teaching a zone was to introduce the players to the sliding movements and break them of the habit of guarding one particular opponent on defense. They had to learn to make their first movement in the direction of the pass and never turn their backs to the ball. Gross stepped down as head coach after the 1954 NCAA Tournament to become a professor in the Physical Education Department at Penn State.

John Egli succeeded Gross and continued the three-decade practice of the Penn State Sliding Zone. He stressed the importance of adapting the basic sliding strategy to combat any type of offense. Egli was a great teacher and helped coaches incorporate the slides into the 2-3, 3-2, and 2-1-2 formations both as an active or passive defense. He wrote the book *Sliding Zone Defense for Winning Basketball*, which is still used by coaches today. Egli became the all-time, most game-winning coach in Penn State basketball history during his 14-year career.

How the Penn State Sliding Zone Arrived in Philadelphia

The city of Philadelphia is recognized as a hotbed for basketball and more specifically as the home of the some of the toughest zone defenses ever played. Coauthor Casey was mentored by two of the games finest zone coaches, Harry Litwack and Jack McCloskey. In 2007, Coach Jack McCloskey was asked, 'When did the Penn State Sliding Zone come to Philadelphia?' Coach McCloskey graciously provided us with the following answer that must be recorded for basketball history.

"It was November 1, 1958, the first official day of basketball practice in the Ivy League, and I was the head coach at the University of Pennsylvania. We had an outstanding young man by the name of Bob Mlky who had excellent skills and was potentially one of the tops players in our school's history. In our second drill, Mlky received a season-ending injury and several days later we lost a second starter. Before these injuries, I had envisioned our players as a running, pressing, and aggressive team. This could no longer be an option. We must slow the game, play zone, and pray that no team would press us.

"Several years earlier, we played Penn State and I was tremendously impressed by their execution of the zone slides and how they adapted to all our offensive moves. The coach of that team was John Egli, a tough competitive man. I knew he was the one coach who could help me. I had learned that John was grieving the loss of his son in a motorcycle accident and I was unsure whether I should ask for his assistance at this time. I did call, and despite his recent loss, he graciously agreed to give me all his knowledge.

"I drove from Philly to State College the following weekend and I spent hours watching films, listening, and learning from the greatest zone defensive coach in the game of basketball. I asked how his zone would play against various offensive moves from A to Z, and he gladly demonstrated an array of moves, many of which were a revelation. I thought I had known something about zone defenses before I had my tutorial sessions with John, but I was dead wrong! John was directly responsible for the University of Pennsylvania's winning season with a starting lineup of three 5'8" guards, a 6'3" forward, and a 6'5" center. I will be forever grateful to this great man. It was his passion for the game of basketball and his complete unselfishness that allowed the Penn State Sliding Zone to come to Philadelphia

"The co-author of this book, Don Casey, spent hours studying the Penn State zone defense. He was a high school coach at the time so he was able to visit our practices, take notes, and incorporate the defensive strategies with his team. I recall one practice session when we switched into our Penn State zone and it created a quick turnover. Suddenly, Coach Casey left his seat in the stands, ran out on the court, and shouted, 'Do it again, Jack.' I laughed and I am sure that John Egli would have loved the moment."

Match-Up Zone Defense

The match-up zone defense was developed to counter the rapid advancement of offensive skills during the 1950s. During this period, the one-hand set shot was replaced by the jump shot; players became skillful dribblers and passers; and coaches created high-powered offenses. It was not uncommon for teams to average over 80 points per game, and no longer could an excellent defender consistently stop even an average offensive player.

The Amoeba Defense

Fran Webster, an assistant coach at Westminster College under legendary Charles "Buzz" Ridl, designed one of the first match-up defenses in the early 1960s. Webster called his defense the "amoeba defense" because he wanted to entice the ball into a corner and then surround it, similar to an amoeba surrounding a food particle before ingesting it. As illustrated in Diagram 2.4, the amoeba differed from conventional zones because its original alignment was a 1-1-2-1. Defensive players X_1 and X_2 set up in a tandem and were the chasers; X_3 and X_4 were the wingmen; and X_5 was the baseman.

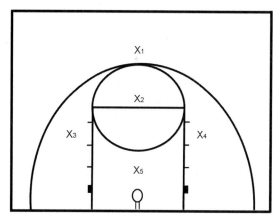

Diagram 2.4 Initial Alignment, the Amoeba Defense

X_1 pressured the ball handler and forced him out of the middle of the floor. X_2 prevented a pass into the high post area. X_3 and X_4 positioned themselves 2 to 3 feet below the foul line extended and were prepared to defend any pass to the wing. X_5 covered the free throw lane area.

The basic premise of Webster's defense was to disrupt the pass, which he believed was the weakest part of the modern player's fundamentals. The amoeba defense attempted to create turnovers by putting pressure on the ball handler as much as possible. There were two fundamental principles in the amoeba defense. The first principle stated that a ball handler had to be pressured as soon as he or she came within 25 feet of the basket. The second principle declared that the ball must be kept out of the "no-ball area." Webster defined this area as being a 15-foot radius around the basket. (See Diagram 2.5.)

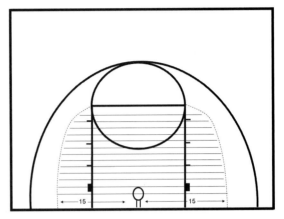

Diagram 2.5 No-Ball Area

Webster's defense controlled the tempo of games and kept teams from running their set patterns. When facing the amoeba, it was so difficult for players to recognize what type of defense was being employed that opposing coaches called it the knuckleball of defenses.

Ridl and Webster moved from Westminster to the University of Pittsburgh and quickly led the Panthers to national prominence. The amoeba defense helped carry Pittsburgh to the Eastern Finals of the NCAA tournament in 1974 and the NIT tournament in 1975.

Former Pittsburgh coach Tim Grgurich took the amoeba defense to the University of Nevada–Las Vegas (UNLV) and spent 12 years as an assistant to Jerry Tarkanian. At UNLV, the element of trapping was added to the amoeba. The Runnin' Rebels reached national prominence during this period by going to the Final Four three times and winning the NCAA title in 1990. Many people only remember the Runnin' Rebels for their fast-breaking offense, but the key to their success was their defense. They attacked and were aggressive. Their defensive intensity forced turnovers and triggered their fast break and high-scoring offense.

The Bill Green Match-Up Zone Defense

In 1962, Bill Green and assistant coach John Males crafted a match-up zone defense using strategies taken from the game of football. After attending a Purdue–Notre Dame football game, Green and Males surmised that football's "monster back" theory could be applied to basketball. Green used the term *rover* instead of *monster back*. The key qualities for a defender to be the rover were quickness, size, and basketball intelligence. It was also important that the rover had the ability to identify offensive alignments and respond to offensive cutters.

Green developed a set of rules for each of the five defensive positions and believed it was crucial to place his personnel in the right positions. He preferred to match up from a 2-1-2 or 2-3 alignment so that his teams were in the best position to rebound and fast break.

The initial alignment for the Bill Green match-up is illustrated in Diagram 2.6. X_1 matched up with the offensive player located at the point. It did not make any difference whether this player had the ball or not. All other defenders reacted to the initial pickup by X_1. X_2 picked up the first offensive player to the left of the point guard. X_3 defended the first

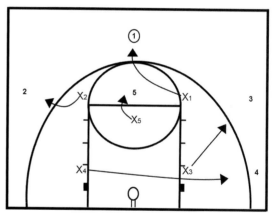

Diagram 2.6 Initial Matchup (Example 1)

offensive player to the right of the point guard. X_4 was the rover and took the second player to the right or left of the point guard. In Diagram 2.6, there was no offensive player on the left side of the floor, so X_4 had to cross the lane and match up with 4 on the right side. X_5's responsibility was to defend the offensive post player.

If there was no offensive player in the post, X_5 defended the player on the baseline to the right of X_1. (See Diagram 2.7.)

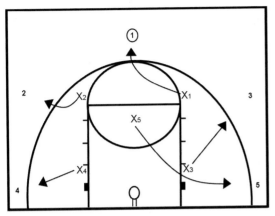

Diagram 2.7 Initial Matchup (Example 2)

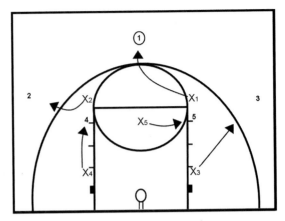

Diagram 2.8 Initial Matchup (Example 3)

Some opponents used a 1-4 offense to combat Green's match-up zone. When this happened, X_5 took the offensive post player positioned at the right elbow. (See Diagram 2.8.)

Green won six Indiana high school state championships using his match-up zone defense. His legendary career included three consecutive state titles at Marion High School from 1985 to 1987.

The Syracuse 2-3 Match-up Zone Defense

When Hall of Fame coach Jim Boeheim played for Syracuse University, the Orangemen were upset by Penn State's sliding zone defense. He was intrigued by the defense and later used many of its concepts to develop a highly successful 2-3 match-up zone. Boeheim's defense creates deflections and turnovers by pressuring the ball handler and trapping whenever possible. Mike Waters from *The Sporting News* said, "Syracuse's 2-3 zone is the Bermuda Triangle; teams venture in and get lost in a sea of arms."

When asked what makes the Syracuse match-up zone so difficult to play against, Big East coach Tom Crean said, "The number one thing is the talented players they have playing the zone. They distort passing lanes with their wingspan and athleticism. They cover a lot of ground, and they do an excellent job of trapping. They play their zone as if they are in a man-to-man."

Boeheim emphasizes the importance of closing out and defending perimeter shooters. Syracuse won the national championship in 2003 when Kansas made only four of 20 attempts from outside the three-point arc. "We pride ourselves on coming out and stopping three-point shooting teams, even though we are playing zone," said Boeheim. "We try to move our zone and be very active in it."

It is the responsibility of the defensive forwards to defend three point shooters at the wing. They must closeout quickly and contest perimeter shots. When there is not a three-point shooter on the wing, the forwards stay in tight and keep the ball out of the post area. Hakim Warrick epitomized the type of forward that makes the Syracuse defense so difficult to attack. His long arms stretched into the passing lanes and altered shots.

His athleticism helped him cover the baseline from the lane to the corner and out to the three-point line at the wing. "You play that area back and forth sort of like a triangle," Warrick said. "You must be able to defend the wing, baseline, and corner. You've got to get out on the wing guy. Giving up a three [three-point shot] right away will get you pulled quickly. If they swing the ball to the wing, you've got to really get out there."

Former Syracuse star player Gerry McNamara described playing the 2-3 zone as hard work. "Our zone defense is active so it is just as tough to play as a man-to-man defense," said McNamara. "It's not like playing a zone in high school."

Besides hard work, the Syracuse defense is built on player communication and trust. As the opponent advances the ball, the defensive guards must decide which player has the ball handler and which player is protecting against a pass into the high post.

The defensive center acts like a middle linebacker and must call out the location of the ball and cutters. It is his responsibility to alert the defensive guards if there is a player coming behind them in the high post. The defensive center must also warn the forwards when there is a shooter running the baseline.

There are six important principles in Boeheim's zone defense:

1. The zone is built on player communication and trust.
2. On every pass, every defender must move and know where to move.
3. All five defenders must stay in their defensive stance.
4. The center must front a low post player.
5. Forwards must cut off the baseline drive and defend against a three-point shot.
6. Always look for opportunities to create deflections and trap the ball handler.

The Zone Defense in Professional Basketball

It took less than two months for the owners in the newly formed Basketball Association of America (BAA) to decide that they wanted no part of the zone defense in their league. The St. Louis Bombers, one of the top teams in the BAA, used a zone defense so successfully that the owners called for a special meeting on January 11, 1947, and voted to prohibit the use of the zone defense. Their reason was that zones were "too effective" in holding the score down, which would hurt fan interest and gate receipts.

In 1949, the BAA merged with the National Basketball League (NBL) and formed the NBA. The NBA continued with the ban on zone defenses until 2001. Jerry Colangelo, one of the most innovative and influential owners in NBA history, believed the approval of the zone defense by the NBA was one of the most significant moves since the implementation of the 24-second shot clock in 1954. "This is a bold move on the part of the NBA to allow something to take place that for years we've been hiding from," said Colangelo. "We feel confident this will enhance the game."

The NBA rules regarding the zone defense are different than the ones used in college and high school basketball. In the NBA, a defensive three-second rule prohibits a defensive player from remaining in the lane for more than three seconds without closely guarding an offensive player.

Many basketball experts believe that the addition of the zone defense in the NBA has allowed coaches more flexibility and augmented their tactical opportunities. Hall of Famer Joe Dumars, president of basketball operations for the Detroit Pistons, believes the zone defense has a definite place in the NBA and that more and more teams will begin utilizing the zone in the future. Prior to the 2007 season, head coach Flip Saunders predicted that the Pistons would use a zone defense at least 10 to 15 percent of the time.

The History of the Zone Press

Successful coaches understand the importance of the zone presses because they can greatly affect the outcome of a game. Some presses are designed to create turnovers while others are used to disrupt the offensive rhythm of an opponent. Coaches utilize different alignments such as the 1-2-1-1 or 2-2-1 and vary the pick-up point between full-court, three-quarter court, and half-court. Studying the history of the zone press provides insight on why zone presses evolved and the role they have played in winning championships.

Pressing Techniques Prior to 1950

Prior to 1950, full-court pressing defense generally occurred only in the closing minutes of a game when the losing team made a last-ditch effort for victory. Pressing at any other time during the game was thought to be fundamentally unsound. Several coaches, such as

Frank Keaney and Gene Johnson, disagreed with this theory and believed in the merit of pressing throughout the entire game.

Frank Keaney and the "Fire Horse Style of Play"

Frank Keaney, the Hall of Fame coach from the University of Rhode Island, developed a style of play called "fire horse basketball," which had his players pressing full court and fast breaking at every opportunity. He developed this system after observing a Boston Bruins' ice hockey game in 1928. Keaney watched quick skaters stab at the puck and make steals before any offense could be mounted, and he was convinced this strategy would also work on the basketball court. Skeptics and traditionalists scorned Keaney's innovative methods, and many coaches and sportswriters called it "crazy basketball."

Keaney proved his critics wrong as he compiled an overall coaching record of 401–124 and led Rhode Island to four NIT tournaments. Keaney's 1921 team stunned the basketball world by scoring 87 points in a single game, a rare occurrence at the time. By the mid-1930s, Rhode Island was known as the "Point-a-Minute" Rams. Many basketball historians call Frank Keaney the "Father of the Fast Break."

Gene Johnson and the 2-2-1 Zone Press

One of the best-kept secrets in basketball was the 2-2-1 zone press. Gene Johnson, the head coach at Wichita University from 1928 to 1933, was introduced to 2-2-1 press during the summer of 1931 when he took his team to Mexico for several exhibition games. He discovered that teams in Mexico played a radically new style of ball that differed greatly from the controlled style used in the United States. Johnson's Wichita team had an advantage in height and size, but the Mexican players harassed the ball handler at all times. Wichita didn't lose too many games during this tour, but its offense was totally disrupted by this new type of pressing defense.

Johnson was so impressed with the 2-2-1 zone press that he incorporated it into his defensive system. He had his players double-team the ball, but at the same time, kept defenders positioned so they would not give up uncontested layups.

"All the other teams in the United States played slow-break basketball, passing the ball back and forth, until you got your men situated," said Johnson. "My theory was, when they brought the ball down and stopped, we went right out and attacked them. We always had the other team's balance upset, because we were the only team in the United States that played that kind of basketball."

"I think it is too bad that nobody has ever given Gene Johnson credit for what he did for college basketball," said Hall of Fame coach Ralph Miller. "Wichita was bothering offenses with the 2-2-1 back in the early 1930s, some 30 years before John Wooden's slick UCLA teams began terrorizing people in the early 1960s. The 2-2-1 was buried in the state of Kansas for a long time. It's always been amazing to me that something as effective as the 2-2-1 press stayed a secret for 20 years."

Pressing Techniques in the 1950s and 1960s

During the decade of the 1950s, four NCAA Division I championship teams employed the press defense as their basic defense—the University of Kansas in 1952, the University of San Francisco in 1955 and 1956, and the University of California in 1959. Their success magnified the potential of pressure defense. Hall of Fame coach John Bunn called the pressing defense "the greatest innovation in basketball since Hank Luisetti set the basketball world agog with his one-handed shot."

Phog Allen and the Kansas Half-Court Pressure Defense

Phog Allen, head coach at Kansas, watched Ralph Miller's Wichita East team win the Kansas high school title in 1951 using the 2-2-1 press. Allen was eager to learn about the press and quizzed Miller for three or four hours about the nuances of his defense. Up to that point, Kansas had never used an organized pressure defense. The following season, Allen incorporated many of the pressure concepts of the 2-2-1 defense into a half-court man-to-man system, and it was an important factor in the Jayhawks' 1952 NCAA National Championship.

But it wasn't until the following year, when Kansas reached the 1953 NCAA Finals with just one starter returning, that the basketball world realized the power of pressure defense. When facing the Jayhawks, it was difficult for an opponent to complete even the simplest pass in the frontcourt. Dean Smith was a player on the Kansas team, and he described their defense as "the first instance of man pressure as we know it today." Hall of Fame coach John Wooden believed it marked "a defensive turning point in basketball."

Elmer Gross and the Penn State 3-2 Sliding Zone Press

In 1954, Penn State surprised the basketball world by snapping Notre Dame's 18-game winning streak and advancing to the Final Four. The Nittany Lions showcased a 3-2 full-court zone press along with their renowned sliding zone defense. The inbounds pass was not contested, but the player receiving the pass was quickly double-teamed, with the hope that he would either throw a bad pass or be unable to advance the ball past the midcourt line in 10 seconds. (See Diagram 2.9.)

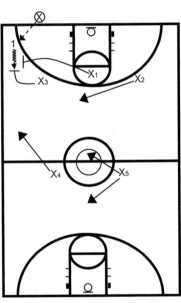

Diagram 2.9 Penn State's 3-2 Sliding Zone Press

The combination of a full-court press and a sliding zone carried Penn State to a third place finish in the NCAA tournament. John Bunn believed the zone press employed by Penn State probably had the greatest influence in popularizing pressing defenses because it received national attention at the 1954 Final Four.

Phil Woolpert and the San Francisco Three-Quarter Court Press

The pressure defense utilized by the University of Kansas in 1952 and 1953 had a great impact on the game of basketball. In the summer of 1953, Hall of Fame coach Phil Woolpert from the University of San Francisco traveled to Kansas and studied the defense with Jayhawk assistant coach Dick Harp. Woolpert incorporated pressure concepts from Kansas with a 2-2-1 zone press that Woolpert had learned as an assistant under Pete Newell when San Francisco won the 1949 NIT title.

Woolpert's San Francisco teams, led by Bill Russell and K.C. Jones, won back-to-back national championships in 1955 and 1956. The year after Russell and Jones graduated, the Dons advanced to the Final Four, where they lost to Kansas and Wilt Chamberlain in the semifinals before beating Michigan State for third place.

San Francisco led the nation in defense on three occasions, and Woolpert was selected twice as National Coach of the Year. His teams won 60 consecutive games from 1955 to 1957, an NCAA record until UCLA's 88-game winning streak took shape in the early 1970s.

Woolpert used two methods when playing the three-quarter-court zone press. In one method, the defender X_1 forced the ball handler to the middle of the court to create a potential trapping situation with X_2. X_4, positioned on the second line of the press, moved up in order to stop a pass being made to 2. Defenders X_3 and X_5 prevented the long passes. X_3, X_4, and X_5 were instructed to go for any ball that they thought they had a 60–40 chance of intercepting. (See Diagram 2.10.)

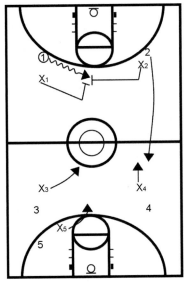

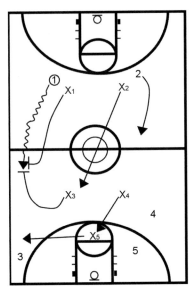

Diagram 2.10 2-2-1 Press (Influence to the Middle)

Diagram 2.11 2-2-1 Press (Influence to the Outside)

In the other method, the defender X_1 forced the dribbler to the outside of the court into a trap just past the half-court line with X_3. X_5 quickly moved to prevent a pass down the sideline to 3. X_2 sprinted back and protected against a pass into the middle of the court. X_4 replaced X_5 and guarded the basket area. (See Diagram 2.11.)

The astute Woolpert believed the success of his defense was directly proportional to the ability, desire, and determination of the players employing it. Woolpert insisted that his front-line defenders sprint back whenever the ball had gone by them. "It's a cardinal sin for a player, once the ball goes by him, to waste any time getting back to the defensive end of the court," said Woolpert. "His first and immediate reaction should be to get back."

Pete Newell and the California 2-2-1 Zone Press

Pete Newell believed that defense started with pressure on the ball. He wanted the front-line defenders in his 2-2-1 zone press to force the ball handler into a trapping situation. The back-line defenders moved into their zone responsibilities and were alert for interceptions. The success of Newell's zone press was the fact that it was a team defense. Every player had to understand his role for the press to be effective. "The front line can do an excellent job in their duties, but it is to no avail if the back line is unresponsive and slow in reacting," said Newell.

As the press defense became more popular in the 1950s, Newell found opponents were better able to attack this type of defense. In 1959, he utilized a supplementary pressure defense that complemented his primary defense. "We had different versions of the press," said Newell. "Right off I might show you a three-quarter press, but all we're doing is trying to determine what your counter is. Then, we'd go to our full-court zone press, which would be the complete opposite of what we'd shown so far. Suddenly, all the defensive responsibilities have changed, and we're much more aggressive than before."

Pete Newell has been recognized as one of the all-time greatest teachers in the game of basketball. "It's amazing the simple way that he teaches," said Duke head coach Mike Krzyzewski. "Everybody's looking for some big discovery, but Pete gets to the heart of things so easily. He points out things that are really easy to see. But I'm wondering, why didn't I see it? It was right in front of me. That's the beauty of Pete. Nobody has ever taught the game as well."

Newell used what today is called the part-whole teaching method. "The parts make the whole," Newell said. "It tells a player why he's doing something. Break it down to one-on-one, two-on-two, and three-on-three. Go through every option of the offense and defense, and the players will understand why you're doing it. And if they make mistakes, you can point it out. The part-whole method can be compared to your car engine. You work on the spark plugs or the carburetor or whatever's causing the problem. You don't have to get rid of the whole motor."

Newell directed the University of California to four consecutive Pacific-8 championships and back-to-back appearances in the NCAA finals in 1959 and 1960. Newell was the first coach in basketball history to win the "Triple Crown" of coaching—NIT championship in 1949, the NCAA championship in 1959, and the Olympic gold medal in 1960.

Jack Ramsay and the St. Joseph 3-1-1 Zone Press

Jack Ramsay developed a ball-hawking style of play that led St. Joseph's University to seven Big 5 championships, 10 postseason tournament appearances, and a third-place finish in the 1965 NCAA Tournament. Ramsay's trademark was a 3-1-1 zone press and an explosive fast-break attack. He utilized the 3-1-1 press as either a full-court press or a half-court press.

Many people have given Ramsay credit for inventing the 3-1-1 press, but he is quick to point out that the recognition should be given to Woody Ludwig at Widener College. In 1949, Ramsay's senior year at St. Joseph's, the Hawks scrimmaged Ludwig's team. "They played a small college schedule and weren't considered a very strong program," said Ramsay. "The scrimmage went easily for St. Joe's until Ludwig applied full-court, zone pressure late in the workout. We had never seen anything like it before and proceeded to turn over the ball frequently. The tactic took us completely out of our game. I tucked away that experience in my memory bank, and when I began my coaching career at St. James High School, I learned all the adjustments Ludwig used in that defense. By the time I was coaching at St. Joseph's, the zone press was part of my defensive game plan—thanks to Woody Ludwig."

In the initial alignment of the 3-1-1 zone press, the front-line defenders X_1, X_2, and X_3 were positioned across the free throw line extended. X_4 was positioned just inside midcourt and looked for the nearest offensive player behind the front line. X_5 set up between the midcourt line and the top of the defensive foul circle and looked for the nearest offensive player. (See Diagram 2.12.)

When the ball was passed inbounds, there was an immediate trap by two front-line players. The trappers (X_1 and X_3) pressured the ball handler and tried to force a lob pass. (See Diagram 2.13.) The other front-line defender (X_2) became the "drifter" and was positioned to intercept the lob pass or stop the give-and-go pass back to the inbounder. X_4 overplayed the deep offensive player on his side of the court. X_5 played between the other offensive players and prevented any long passes.

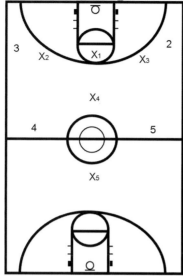

Diagram 2.12 3-1-1 Zone Press

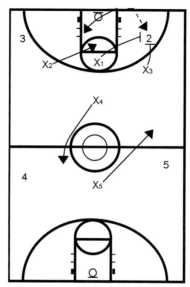

Diagram 2.13 3-1-1 Zone Press Trap

Once the ball was advanced past midcourt, Ramsay had his team stay in a half-court 3-1-1 press. The rules for the half-court press were similar to the full-court press. The defenders looked to double-team the ball and create turnovers, which would result in fast-break opportunities for St. Joseph's.

Ramsay believed there were eight important principles for the zone press:

1. Pressure the ball handler.
2. Trap whenever possible.
3. Force an opponent into a "bad-pass" position.
4. Force the ball handler into a held-ball situation.
5. Intercept or deflect every pass possible.
6. Look to steal the ball at all times.
7. Defenders not involved in a trap must slough off and protect the most vulnerable areas
8. Hustle and exert constant pressure on the opponent, but do not foul.

John Wooden and the UCLA 2-2-1 Zone Press

John Wooden won the first of his 10 national championships in 1964 using a 2-2-1 zone press. Wooden selected this press because it: (1) maximized the strengths of UCLA's key players; (2) increased the tempo of the game against ball-control teams; (3) highlighted the quickness of the UCLA defenders; and (4) neutralized the opponent's height advantage (UCLA did not have a starter taller than 6′5″).

UCLA used the 2-2-1 press after they scored. "This defense was not designed to take the ball away from the opposition nearly as much as to force them into mental and physical errors on which we hoped to capitalize," said Wooden. "We felt if we kept constant pressure on them, they would be forced to "hurry" their offense, which would be in direct contrast to the style of game that they normally played."

Wooden identified five keys for success in the 2-2-1 zone press:

1. Do not reach in when defending a ball handler.
2. Direct a dribbler into a trap.
3. Permit only lob or bounce passes forward.
4. As soon as the ball passes your individual line of defense, turn and sprint toward your defensive basket and pick up the most dangerous open player.
5. If no opponent is in your zone, move toward the zone that is being attacked.

One of Wooden's assistants, Denny Crum, implemented the 2-2-1 press into his defensive system at the University of Louisville, and it was the catalyst for NCCA national championships in 1980 and 1986. Crum coached the Cardinals from 1971 to 2001 and led Louisville to 23 NCAA tournaments and six Final Four appearances.

Crum believed that defense was the most important part of the game. His basketball philosophy was to pressure opponents for 40 minutes. Crum utilized full-court, three-quarter court, and half-court presses. He emphasized the importance of not fouling during the press. Once the ball handler was stopped, Crum wanted his players to stay one arm's length away. The closer the defenders got to the trapped player, the easier it was for the ball handler to get out of the trap.

"I learned from Coach Wooden that the by-products of the press are far more valuable than the press itself," said Crum. "The reason his teams pressed was not to steal the ball but rather to dictate the tempo of the game."

Other by-products of the press included:

- Players love to press and fans love to watch it.
- A press at the beginning of the game can cause a turnover, which relaxes your players and puts extra pressure on your opponents.
- Pressing requires your players to be in excellent physical condition.
- It allows a coach to use more players.
- It teaches anticipation, which is carried over to other defensive plays.
- When you press, your players are prepared to attack a press, because they play against it every day.
- Most important, the press sets the tempo and edges your opponents out of their offensive strategies, forcing them to do things they don't normally do.

Neal Baisi and the Pressing Defense

Neal Baisi's football background helped him revolutionize the game of basketball with a pressing defense. "I had played a lot of football, and not once did we start to play defense at the 50-yard line," said Baisi. "So I thought, why not play defense all over the court in basketball. That's how the concept started."

Baisi believed offensive teams were becoming so proficient at scoring that it was essential for coaches to press in order to keep an opponent off-balance. He also felt there was an "economic advantage" to pressing because it created turnovers that led to fast-break points. Baisi's 1955 squad at West Virginia Tech was the first colle-giate team to average over 100 points per game. During the Baisi era, six of his teams led the nation in scoring, and many of these points were generated from steals off the pressing defense.

Baisi's defensive motto was: "The difficult takes time; the impossible a little longer." He pushed his players to do more than they thought was possible. Baisi demanded the maximum effort from every player, every minute on the court. His innovative training techniques included having his players wear rubber boots during many of the drills to increase their quickness and agility.

Baisi led his West Virgina Tech teams to four conference championships and a record of 263–82 over a 12-year period. In 1961, he authored the classic textbook entitled *Coaching the Zone and Man-to-Man Pressing Defenses*, which is still used as a reference by coaches today.

Pressing Techniques in Today's Game

Today, all the game's greatest coaches have recognized the value of pressing. It has been used both as a tool to speed up the tempo of the game or to slow it down, depending upon the game. Winning coaches have made pressing an important part of their defensive philosophy and realized that a press will only be as good as the amount of time that one practices it.

Since 2000, coaches such as Jim Calhoun (Connecticut), Gary Williams (Maryland), and Billy Donovan (Florida) have won NCAA national championships using pressing defenses. Calhoun's three-quarter court 2-2-1 press has been referred to as a "safe press" because three defenders were positioned behind the trap, and they had less ground to cover to get back to their half-court defense. As shown in Diagram 2.14, the Huskies put their two best "on-the-ball" defend-

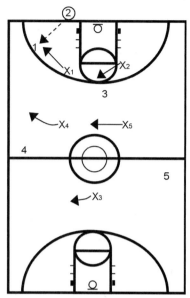

Diagram 2.14 UConn's 2-2-1 Zone Press

ers, X_1 and X_2, in the front line so they could pressure the ball handler and force him up the sideline. Defenders X_4 and X_5 were on the second line, where they contained the dribbler on the sideline and trapped. Whenever the ball was passed away from them, X_4 and X_5 rotated back and covered the basket. X_3 played from one sideline to the other and was usually the best anticipator and interceptor.

Calhoun reinforced seven key principles in his press:

1. Put pressure on the ball.
2. Force the ball to a sideline.
3. Contain the dribbler and keep the ball out of the middle.
4. Emphasize the 1-4 principle—one defender on the ball and four defenders in good, balanced help positions.
5. After the ball is funneled into a trap, each defender must rotate and make the proper defensive adjustments.
6. Challenge every shot.
7. Rebound—limit second-shot opportunities.

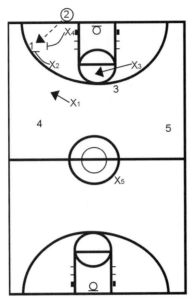

Diagram 2.15 1-2-1-1 Zone Press

Maryland won the 2002 NCAA Championship using a 1-2-1-1 zone press. As shown in Diagram 2.15, the Terrapins trapped the first pass in the corner with X_4 and X_2. Defenders X_1 and X_3 became the interceptors, and X_5 was the safetyman. It was usually a "one and done" trap back to their half-court defense. The 1-2-1-1 press was most vulnerable to a pass over the top because three defenders were behind the ball in transition.

Pressing has changed a lot during the past 25 years. The reason for this is very simple. Players start seeing the press at a very young age, and they have grown accustomed to it. No longer does the press have the psychological effect that it once did, but it is just as important. Today's successful coaches design their pressure defenses according to their personnel and what they want to get out of it. They realize that it will not always get them a steal, but it will produce deflections, hurried shots, shooting from spots on the court that the opponent would not normally shoot from, and better rebounding situations. Pressing helps take the ball out of the hands of an opponent's primary scorers and best ball handlers. It often forces the opposition to do something that it doesn't want to do. It makes the offense pass more often than they normally do and use more of the shot clock.

3

Establishing a Defensive Mind-Set

From the moment players are introduced to the game of basketball, they immediately fall in love with the offensive aspects of the game, such as shooting and dribbling. This gets reinforced further when they begin playing games, and one of the first questions asked after a contest is, "How many points did you score?" No one ever asks, "What kind of defensive game did you have?"

At practice, watch a player when he or she first steps onto the court. Almost every player will immediately retrieve a ball and then begin working on shooting techniques. It would be a notable occasion if one would see a player working on his or her individual defense.

Because of the natural attraction that a player has for offense, coaches have a difficult challenge in instilling the defensive mindset that is necessary for team success. Chapter 3 presents the keys for creating a defensive state of mind that will enable your players to contest shots, stop penetration, deny passes, dive for loose balls, secure rebounds, and create turnovers.

Requirements for the Individual Defender

Whether it's in the NBA, college, or high school basketball, the one thing that is necessary to win consistently is a commitment to playing strong defense both as a team and as an individual. Bob Knight, the most game-winning collegiate coach in men's basketball, said, "The very first thing that has to be done to win, in any team sport, is playing well defensively."

Many players do not understand that defense is a state of mind, an attitude. A player's desire, determination, and discipline are more important than his or her natural talents. When asked what makes a good defender, Lute Olson said, "Desire, dedication, mental alertness, foot quickness, and great physical conditioning."

Hall of Fame coach Pete Carrill believed defense involved three things – courage, energy, and intelligence. Bud Presley, former coach at Menlo Junior College (California) and defensive consultant to the Golden State Warriors, said, "I have coached and seen a great number of young men who, though lacking in outstanding natural ability, have become exceptional defensive players through desire and intense effort. For good defense is only about 20 percent technique. The other 80 percent is measured by your desire to succeed."

Desire

"Team defense is as good as the desire of the players," said Hall of Fame coach William "Red" Holzman. The chant "DEE-fense! DEE-fense!" echoed through New York's Madison Square Garden in the early 1970s as Holzman led the Knicks to two NBA championships. Holzman turned the Knicks into relentless, aggressive, defensive-minded players. They pressured opposing guards, created turnovers, and positioned themselves to help a teammate whenever necessary.

Morgan Wootten, who compiled a record of 1,274–192 during his high school coaching career, identified desire as a key component in his defensive system. "Defense is played with the mind, heart, and feet," said Wootten. "The mind tells you what to do, the heart gives you the desire, and the feet put you in the proper position to execute it."

Regardless of a player's natural talent, he or she will not excel on defense unless there is a strong desire to stop an opposing team from scoring. One way for a coach to aid in the development of a defender's desire is to challenge that player's character and toughness in regard to stopping an opposing player. The first step is to instill personal responsibility for individual defense. It should be an insult to a defender's pride whenever he or she plays poor defense. The second step is to instill collective responsibility for team defense so that every member of the team feels responsible for stopping an opponent from scoring. When this occurs, a team's defensive pride is emerging, and great things will happen.

Another method of instilling desire is to sell the importance of never letting a teammate down. If taught properly, this will eventually become a team's driving force and its identity. This principle is discussed almost every day in Tom Crean's program at Marquette University. Players are held accountable for making their teammates successful. NBA player and former Marquette star Travis Diener said, "We quickly learned if one player wasn't doing his job, then he was hurting the whole team. In Marquette's program, no one wanted to bring the team down."

The transformation of a group of individuals into a strong defensive unit does not happen automatically. The strength of any team is a direct result of its leaders. A coach can nourish his or her team's desire to play defense by emphasizing the importance of defense and rewarding outstanding defensive efforts. Jud Heathcote, who led Michigan State to the NCAA championship in 1979, always said, "You will get what you emphasize. If you want to be an outstanding defensive team, it must be emphasized every day."

Determination

Great defenders find a way to succeed regardless of the obstacles that are placed in their path. This driving force is called determination. Determined defenders are mentally and physically tough. They never give up or settle for anything less than their best effort. They know there are no short cuts to success—it takes hours and hours of hard work. When a group of players are committed to making the maximum defensive effort every time they take the floor, they have an opportunity to win any game.

Determination is reflected by a player's effort, competitiveness, and aggressiveness. Outstanding defenders not only play hard, but they also demonstrate the personal courage to compete every second on the court regardless of the time left in the game or the score.

Aggressiveness is characterized by a strong will to dominate an opponent. "For us to win," said Bob Knight, "we feel that our defense must dominate the offense. Our defense is built on aggressiveness. This idea permeates all of our defensive thinking, and our players are well aware of this. We believe, that while not everyone can be quick, or big, or strong, there is no reason why each of our players can't be extremely aggressive."

Too often, defensive players are only taught how to react to an offensive player's moves or fakes instead of being aggressive and forcing the action. Examples of aggressiveness are pressuring the ball handler, diving for loose balls, taking charges, fighting over screens, stopping cutters, blocking out, and pursuing all missed shots.

An excellent gauge for aggressiveness is the number of fifty-fifty balls recovered during the course of a game. *A fifty-fifty ball* is a term given to a loose ball or missed shot that both teams have almost an equal chance of retrieving. The team with the most hustle and aggressiveness will consistently win this battle.

Tenacious defense has been one of the staples of Phil Martelli's teams at Saint Joseph's. "The first thing I recruit is a guy who is willing to compete," said Martelli. "Second, I want a player who loves basketball. Lastly, I want to have a player who will strive for greatness and allow us to coach him to greatness. Unfortunately, there are a lot of young players who know it all. I want a player who realizes that coaching is a big part of his improvement. Someone who is willing to dare to be great."

Discipline

Coach Mike Krzyzewski defines discipline as "doing what you are supposed to do in the best possible manner at the time you are supposed to do it." Krzyzewski believes it is a coach's responsibility to instill the discipline of personal responsibility, honesty, and respect for authority.

Defense requires strong discipline. Disciplined defenders direct their thoughts and actions toward the desired goal. They stay focused and concentrate on the job that must be done, even under adverse conditions. They demonstrate discipline in being able to pressure opponents without fouling and putting them on the free throw line. They form a close-knit unit with their teammates based on collective responsibility. Nothing great is ever achieved without discipline.

Requirements for Team Defense

Team defense was the cornerstone for Dean Smith's North Carolina basketball program. "By team defense we meant having a solidarity that required each player to trust his teammates," said Smith. "Our defense would not work if one player was out of position."

It takes five players moving together as one single unit for maximum results. Veteran NBA coach Ron Adams believes defensive players should be taught to visualize themselves as being tied to a highly elastic cord, which unites each defender and also encompasses the ball. As players move and the ball moves, defensive players are required to make adjustments. Adams describes the cord that connects the players as being filled with a special kind of sustaining elixir. "This fluid circulates and thus permeates each participant in a most unusual manner," said Adams. "For it imparts to each defender unselfishness, altruism, and a sense of commitment to the task at hand. It gives collective strength to each person and thus encourages an understanding of we are all responsible for the lot of the other."

Successful coaches begin teaching and preaching defense the first moment they meet with their team. Players should be told from the very start that the key to team success lies in the ability of the team to become a tenacious defensive unit. Two essential ingredients for this to happen are teamwork and a positive attitude for team defense.

Teamwork

No team will be successful without teamwork no matter how many All-Americans it has. There are two elements that are necessary for effective teamwork. First, the team members must share a common objective, one that is important enough to them that they are willing to make sacrifices in order to achieve it. Second, team members must care about each other in a way that leads to selflessness and a common concern for others on the team.

"When the players on a team commit themselves to one another to be a cohesive defensive unit, they get the feeling like that of an army going to war together," said veteran NBA coach Del Harris. "They feel they are part of something that each can be proud of. They have spirit and camaraderie. And they have a team that plays consistently well."

Teamwork was the driving force for the Green Bay Packers' success in the 1960s. Coach Vince Lombardi took over a last-place team and built it into one of the most dominant National Football League (NFL) teams of all time, winning five NFL championships over a seven-year span. "Teamwork is what the Green Bay Packers were all about," said Lombardi. "They didn't do it for individual glory, they did it because they loved one another."

In 2006, the Miami Heat shocked the basketball world by winning the NBA championship with a team composed of players who most basketball experts thought would implode because of poor team chemistry. Coach Pat Riley masterfully crafted his defense and offense around 15 team members. The players took ownership of Riley's motto "15 Strong" and refused to buckle during adverse times. "We have a faith-based team here," said Riley. "You must have faith in each other and believe in what you are doing in order to summon the courage and perseverance that it takes to be a champion."

After Miami lost the first two games of the NBA finals to Dallas, almost everyone had written them off. But the Heat stormed back and won the next four games because they stayed together and never gave up. Most Valuable Player of the NBA finals Dwyane Wade talked about the importance of persevering through tough times. "To me, it's the bad moments that make a person," said Wade. "You're going to fall. It's how you get up that defines you. Anybody can be great in life when things are going good. What about when things are going bad? This is what I like because this is how I'll know what kind of team I have. That's going to decide whether we're a championship team and whether I'm a good player or great."

Positive Attitude for Team Defense

A positive defensive attitude must be promoted with your players. They have to believe that defense will win games for them and take pride in accomplishing their defensive objectives.

A positive attitude for team defense elevates a squad to the point where the whole is greater than the sum of its parts. In other words, the collective effort of five defenders working together is far greater than the sum of five individual efforts. This phenomenon is often referred to as "synergy." Author Stephen Covey described synergy in mathematical terms as $1 + 1 = 3$ or more.

The Detroit Pistons reigned as the 2004 NBA Champions because they combined their individual strengths to compensate for individual shortcomings. The Pistons soundly defeated the Los Angeles Lakers, one of the most glamorous collections of superstars ever, because every player was on the same page and played together as a single unit. Joe Dumars, Detroit's president of basketball operations, agreed that a positive team attitude was the deciding factor in the NBA finals. "I know that they (Los Angeles) had the two best players in the world (Shaquille O'Neal and Kobe Bryant), but this is not a tennis match, it is basketball," said Dumars.

Selling Defense to Your Team

We believe that defense is the most efficient method of building a true team. Successful coaches devise methods to sell the power of defense to their players and to the general public. Listed next are ways that coaches can promote the importance of defense.

Create a Defensive Mission Statement

One of the best ways to get your players headed toward the same goal is to create a defensive mission statement that is understood by all your players. Keep the mission statement relatively short, and use words that are clear and explicit. Consider having your defensive mission statement displayed on a sign in your locker room, or put it inside of each player's locker.

An example of a defensive mission statement used by coauthor Pim at Limestone College is: To develop tenacious defenders with an aggressive mindset who are committed to stopping opponents from scoring on each possession of every game.

Use Visual Images

Successful coaches have a clear vision for their team defense and know what it should look like before they even begin. It is then the coach's responsibility to unite the players and get them to believe and commit to his or her vision.

Defensive highlight tapes, pictures, and motivational signs are an excellent way to reinforce a team's defensive vision. At Marquette University, there are constant reminders everywhere, from the hallways to the locker room, the film room to the showers. The moment a player walks through the front door of the gymnasium he sees images and motivational sayings that portray the tradition, pride, and core values of Marquette basketball. There are also pictures of players diving for loose balls, communicating on defense, and contesting shots.

"Initially the motivational signs are things players look at and read," explained Travis Diener. "Then at some point, each player internalizes the meaning of the words. Eventually, a player begins living out these values in everything he does both on and off the court."

Many coaches create defensive highlight tapes illustrating what "right looks like." It is an excellent way to reinforce outstanding defensive play and build team pride. For example, if one of the core principles for your defense is to eliminate second shots, make a tape of a series of possessions where all five of your players are blocking out and pursuing the missed shot. Use the film session to accentuate the positive rather than always showing players making mistakes.

Assess Individual and Team Defense

It is important to establish a defensive grading system to help your players understand both the positive and negative aspects of individual and team defense. NBA coach Don Nelson designed a defensive assessment that appraises each defender on every possession during a game. Nelson started the defensive grading system in Dallas, and although he's tweaked some specifics for Golden State, the basics remain the same.

When a defensive player makes a mistake, such as being out of position or not contesting a shot, he receives a negative mark. More than one mark can be given on a single possession, so if two players are out of place, that's two mistakes. All the negatives are then added together and weighted against the number of possessions in a game to determine a final ratio of correct coverage. The higher the percentage, the more the Warriors have followed their defensive game plan.

A score of 70 is considered outstanding; anything under 55 is a red flag. The Warriors aim to score in the upper 60s. Players are not graded individually, but they do receive a report that includes the number of mistakes they contributed toward lowering the overall score.

Set Defensive Performance Goals

Do your players have a clear understanding of what they need to do defensively in order for the team to be successful? What defensive performance goals have you set for your team? Listed below are examples of critical areas that should be reinforced with specific goals.

- **Consecutive Stops.** At Marquette, Coach Tom Crean believes one of the keys to winning is stopping your opponent three or more possessions in a row because it gives your offense an opportunity to make a run. Marquette's goal is to make three consecutive defensive stops at least seven times during a game.

- **Deflections.** Over the past decade, many coaches have been charting deflections and stressing their importance. Whenever a defender touches the ball, there is a chance that one of his or her teammates might steal it as a result. Deflections create easy scoring opportunities and give the defense a decided edge in the psychological battle. The goal at Marquette is to get a minimum of 35 deflections every game. This goal was adjusted to 40 per game in 2003 for their Final Four team that included three future NBA players (Dwyane Wade, Travis Diener, and Steve Novak).

- **Steals.** Steals create additional scoring opportunities for your offense and serve as a great momentum builder. Pat Summitt and her Tennessee Lady Vols have established a goal of 12 or more steals per game.

- **Turnovers.** Turnovers are similar to steals in that they are missed opportunities for an offensive team to score. The goal for the Lady Vols at Tennessee is 20 or more forced turnovers.

- **Opponent's Free Throws.** Keeping your opponent off the free throw line is one of the most important factors in determining the winning and losing team in basketball. The 2006 NBA Finals confirmed this theory as the victorious Miami Heat averaged 34.5 free throw attempts while Dallas only went to the free throw line 25.8 times per game. An excellent goal is to permit your opponent 15 or fewer free throw attempts per game.

4

Basic Training

Throughout the history of basketball, players and coaches have concentrated more on offensive skills and often neglected the defensive fundamentals. As a result, it often takes a period of time before the defense can catch up to the latest offensive trends. An example of this is the Princeton offense, which was created by Hall of Fame coach Pete Carril. This offense featured backdoor cuts that resulted in wide-open layup shots that embarrassed even the best defenders. Princeton frustrated and occasionally upset some of the nation's top teams using their acclaimed offense. No top-ranked team wanted to face Carril's well-drilled Princeton squad in the NCAA tournament.

Over the past 10 years, a number of teams have incorporated many of Carril's tactics into their offenses. As a result, defenses have had more opportunities to prepare and play against the Princeton offense and have become better at defending many of its options.

To lessen the advantage that an offense has over a defense, coaches must establish basic defensive concepts that remain constant no matter what offense an opponent is running. Always remember that a fundamentally sound defensive team will be more consistent than a team relying predominantly on its offensive skills. Very seldom does a defensive team have an "off night."

Chapter 4 is entitled "Basic Training" because it identifies core defensive concepts that serve as the foundation for defensive success. It also provides lead-up drills that will help players acquire on-the-ball defensive skills. These skills will help defenders become excellent team players in a zone defense.

Defensive Concepts

There are seven concepts that should be the heart of your defensive system and the foundation of your defensive philosophy. Any defense, whether zone or man-to-man, must be built on the following concepts: (1) sprint back, (2) communicate, (3) keep the ball out of the red zone, (4) crowd the ball handler, (5) control penetration, either by the dribble or the pass, (6) contest all shots, and (7) eliminate second shots.

1. Sprint Back

The most important part of defense is how quickly a team converts from offense to defense. Many teams are slow getting back on defense because coaches neglect emphasizing this area. Excellent defensive teams do not give up fast-break baskets.

The first zone defensive concept is to sprint back and make the offense face five defenders every possession. Do not allow the offense to have an outnumbering situation such as a two-on-one or a three-on-two. Defensive transition must be a top priority every day.

The key points in transition defense are:

- Anticipate the fast break on every possession.
- Always sprint back on defense.
- See the ball as you sprint back.
- Look over the inside shoulder to prohibit any pass being thrown over your head.
- Never allow the offensive team to outnumber you.
- Communicate with teammates as you sprint back on defense.
- Protect the basket area and stop all fast-break layups.
- Get into your zone defense quickly and always see the ball.

2. Communicate

Communication is the glue that holds the zone defense together. There is no close second to team members talking with one another on defense. It is an ongoing process and one of the most challenging parts of building a team defense. Getting players to talk on the court must be reinforced every day.

Red Holzman, the NBA Coach of the Decade for the 1970s, had his players continually talking on defense because he believed that "basketball is a game where the use of the mind, body, and voice are equally important." Talking on defense helped the New York Knicks win NBA titles in 1970 and 1973. Longtime NBA coach Del Harris believes there has never been a great "silent defense."

The following are important teaching points for improving communication on defense:

- Use a common language of short terms or phrases.
- Alert teammates to all screens and cutters.
- Require players to communicate in every defensive drill.
- Improving communication on the court must be a top priority every day.

3. Keep the Ball out of the Red Zone

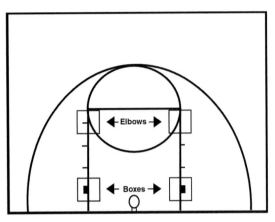

Diagram 4.1 The Red Zone

The most dangerous areas on the floor are the elbows and the boxes. (See Diagram 4.1.) Any time the offensive team has the ball in these areas, the defense is very vulnerable. Defensive success depends on keeping the ball out of the red zone.

Key points in keeping the ball out of the box and the elbow are:

- Forbid direct passes to the box by having an arm and a leg in the passing lane.
- Stop direct passes to the elbow by having active feet and hands.
- Always see the ball and anticipate cutters.
- Prohibit offensive players from making a straight-line cut into either the box or the elbow.

4. Crowd the Ball Handler

The cornerstone of any defense is pressure on the ball. It is the most important individual defensive concept. The object of the defensive team is to force the opponent to move under continuous pressure. Crowd the ball handler, and do not allow unobstructed looks, called "comfort looks," at the basket.

The key points in crowding the ball handler are:

- Be close enough to the ball handler to obstruct his or her view of the basket.
- Maintain constant pressure, and do not allow comfort looks at the basket.
- Keep the hands active. Active hands create deflections.
- Distort the ball handler's ability to see the floor.

- Always stay between the ball handler and the basket. This is called either the ball-you-basket principle or the buttocks-to-the-baseline rule.

5. Control Penetration Either by the Dribble or the Pass

One of the most difficult jobs of defending a ball handler is to apply pressure but at the same time control dribble penetration. The key to success is to stay balanced and maintain the proper spacing from the offensive player.

The best way to maintain proper spacing is to use a retreat step whenever the ball handler makes a fake. A defender executes the retreat step by pushing off the front foot, taking a step backward with the rear foot, and then sliding the front foot back to reestablish position and balance. The defender is simply retreating 6 inches and creating a cushion with the ball handler. Too often, defenders react to a fake by moving laterally, which results in the defensive player getting beat by a crossover move.

We classify on-the-ball defenders into three categories. Good defensive players can defend one dribble without getting beat by penetration. Very good defensive players can defend two dribbles. Superior defenders can control the ball and make the ball handler pick up his or her dribble.

When defending a player without the ball, always see both the ball and your player. Maintain a floor position so that you can help a teammate that gets beat by dribble penetration, and at the same time, be prepared to block an offensive player's cut toward the ball. Never let a player cut in front of your face. Block the cut and force the offensive player to change his or her path.

The key principles in controlling penetration either by the dribble or the pass are:

- When guarding a player who still has the option of dribbling, respect all fakes by using a retreat step.

- When defending a dribbler, always stay between the ball handler and the basket.
- Stop dribble penetration to the basket. Make the ball handler dribble in an arc rather than a straight line to the basket.
- When defending a cutter, never let the offensive player cut in front of your face.
- Force cutters to change their path. Block the cut.

6. Contest All Shots

Every shot must be contested. This lowers opponents' shooting percentages and increases a team's chances for victory. In a 2005 study by Pim, Coughlin, Fielitz, and Fry, 477 Division I conference games were analyzed to determine which statistical factors were the most important in determining the winning and losing teams. The team with the lower field-goal shooting percentage was the eventual loser in 356 of 477 games, or 74.6 percent of the time.

The key teaching points when contesting a shot are:

- Don't leave the floor until the shooter does.
- Fully extend the lead arm on all shots.
- Keep the lead hand in a vertical position with the wrist back. Do not swat at the shot.
- Apply verbal pressure by shouting "Shot!"

7. Eliminate Second Shots

Successful basketball teams do not allow their opponent second-shot opportunities. They keep offensive players from securing rebounds by blocking out and then pursuing the ball. Dean Lockwood from the University of Tennessee Lady Vols calls this technique "hit and get." In other words, the defender must make the "first hit" after the shot is taken, and then quickly go after the ball.

Tom Crean, the highly successful coach from Marquette University, believes that a team will score on 50 percent of their second-shot attempts and 80 percent of their third-shot attempts. Because of these high percentages, Crean works on blocking out every day in practice. One of his favorite teaching tools is a rebounding dome that fits over the top of the basket and prevents any shots from going inside the hoop. It helps players learn how to anticipate that every shot may be missed. As a constant reminder of Crean's emphasis on rebounding, the dome was taken with the team on road trips during the 2007 season, and it was even brought into the team's huddle during certain games.

The most important principle in zone defensive rebounding is to not allow any opponent positioned in your assigned area to secure a missed shot. If all five defenders do their job, there will be no second-shot opportunities. Hall of Fame coach Chuck Daly believes that blocking out is the single most difficult thing to sell to your players.

Mental and physical toughness are key components of successful rebounding because the missed shot does not always go to the tallest player or the one who can jump the highest. The majority of the time it goes to the player who wants the ball the most. Mentally tough rebounders refuse to quit in their attempt to secure a missed shot. They take charge of their assigned area and make sure that no offensive player gets the ball in that particular location.

George Raveling, former coach at Washington State, Iowa, and Southern California, wrote the first book solely devoted to the art of rebounding in 1972 entitled *War on the Boards*. Raveling described rebounding as physical combat and taught his players to play with reckless abandon. He believed that rebounding was 75 percent desire and 25 percent ability. "In my opinion," said Raveling, "rebounding comes down to one basic fact of life—how much do you want the ball? A rebounder has only three friends and their names are desire, courage, and aggressiveness. I want my rebounders to be hostile, mobile, and agile."

Defensive players must be aware of when and where a shot is taken and remember that the longer the shot, the longer the

Opponents must be blocked out in order to eliminate second-shot opportunities.

rebound. Plus, a missed shot from the wing or corner will be re-bounded on the weak side approximately 70 percent of the time.

Key points in eliminating second shots are:

- Assume that every shot will be missed.
- Block out and get the inside rebounding position.
- Make the first contact—put your body on an opponent.
- Pursue the missed shot—attack the rebound.
- Go to the boards with your hands up.
- Secure the rebound with two hands.
- Rebound with a passion.
- Long shots result in long rebounds.

Building Your Defense

Our defense is developed through the whole-part-whole method. We teach the bedrock defensive concepts, show the desired end state, and then work on breakdown drills. It is a fact that team defense will only be as good as the individual defensive skills of the players on your team. The best way to teach team defense is through a step-by-step process starting with individual techniques.

A prerequisite for any successful zone defense is strong man-to-man defensive fundamentals. Becoming proficient in man-to-man defense will develop habits that can be transferred to any type of defense. Therefore, it is essential to begin each season with man-to-man defensive drills even if you do not believe this will be your primary defense. Some coaches tend to overlook the importance of the fundamentals and do not spend enough time teaching the basics.

Basketball is a game of balance and quickness. Players must be able to accelerate, change directions, and stop abruptly while maintaining their balance. Coach John Wooden considered two of the most important attributes of a player were quickness under control and team attitude. "Be quick—but don't hurry" was one of Wooden's favorite phrases because he believed basketball must be played fast but never out of control. Two components of quickness are concentration and anticipation. Both must be developed if players are to become excellent defenders.

Balance is the foundation upon which good individual defense is built. A player with poor balance is easily beaten by dribble penetration and is prone to excessive fouling. Personal fouls and made free throws were two of the top three statistical factors that predicted team success in college basketball during the 2005 season. The team that committed the higher number of personal fouls was the eventual loser in 75 percent of the games.

On-the-Ball Defensive Fundamentals

The starting point for building your defense should be to teach the basic fundamental of guarding a player with the ball. Three essential components of on-the-ball defense are the stance, footwork, and slides.

Defensive Stance

Developing a strong defensive foundation is important because a defender's success is dependent on his or her ability to react instantly in any direction. The first phase in developing your defense is to teach the defensive stance when guarding a ball handler. Pat Summitt uses the teaching phrase "high hands, low hips, quick feet" to teach the stance at the University of Tennessee.

The teaching of the defensive stance is broken into the following five basic parts: head, back, legs, feet, and hands.

Head. The prerequisite for defense is a well-balanced stance. The position of the head determines body balance. Key teaching points are:

- Keep the chin up and position the head over the midpoint of the feet.
- Eyes should be focused on the ball handler's midsection.

Back. The alignment of the back is important because it controls the position of the defender's head. Key teaching points are:

- Keep the back fairly straight.
- Do not bend at the waist.

Legs. Defense is never played with straight legs. It is our goal to have all five defenders in the proper floor position with their knees bent at all times. Key teaching points are:

- Keep the knees bent and maintain a low center of gravity.
- Get low by bending the knees and lowering the buttocks.

Feet. Excellent defenders have active feet and know that the feet are the primary tool for playing defense. Key teaching points are:

- Keep the feet slightly wider than the shoulders.
- Distribute the weight evenly on the whole foot.
- Position the feet in either a staggered or parallel stance.

The defensive stance is the foundation for defensive success.

Hands. Active hands create deflections, and deflections are the barometer of aggressive defense. They reflect your players' intensity. When Hubie Brown was coaching the Memphis Grizzlies, he had a goal of getting at least seven deflections in each quarter. Key teaching points are:

- Keep the hands and arms at waist level or higher.
- Keep the elbows flexed and arms close to the body.

Defensive Footwork

There are three defensive steps that must be mastered by defenders. These are the retreat step, the advance step, and the swing step. Do not underestimate the importance of the three steps. They are the key to maintaining pressure on the ball and containing the dribbler.

Morgan Wootten, the Naismith Foundation High School Coach of the Twentieth Century, created defensive drills that employed the retreat, advance, and swing steps every day in practice. During his career, Wootten compiled the all-time best record and the highest winning percentage among high school coaches.

Retreat Step. The retreat step is the antidote to defending against the all-important first step of an offensive player with the ball. As previously discussed, when an opponent makes a fake or a move toward the basket, the defender executes a retreat step. This creates the proper spacing between the ball handler and the defender and prevents the defensive player from getting beat with the crossover move. Another time to use the retreat step is when the dribbler turns his or her back to you. This will create a cushion and keep the ball handler from using a drop step to spin past you. Key teaching points are:

- Push the front foot into the floor and simultaneously take a step backward with the rear foot.
- Do not lift the front foot off the floor—slide it back.
- Create a cushion from the ball handler.

Advance Step. The advance step is a difficult skill to master. A defender must be able to advance and put pressure on a ball handler without losing his or her balance. Key teaching points are:

- Push with the back foot and slide the front foot toward the ball handler.
- Bring the hand that corresponds with the front foot up to the ball handler's face.
- Keep the weight back.
- Be prepared to push off the front foot and step backward with the rear foot to execute a retreat step.

Swing Step. The swing step is the defensive technique to counter the ball handler's use of the crossover step. It is designed to create a cushion between the ball handler and the defender so that the defensive player does not get beat by penetration. Key teaching points are:

- Lock the shoulder of the arm corresponding with the direction of the ball handler.
- Swing the elbow of the locked shoulder in the direction that you want to go. Subsequently, the action of the elbow forces the body to quickly move the front leg in the direction of the ball handler and prevents getting beat by penetration.

De Matha's "Hey" Drill

Hall of Fame coach Morgan Wootten at De Matha High School designed this drill. The components of the "Hey" drill are the advance step, the retreat step, and the swing step. The squad forms three lines across the floor facing the coach, who is standing on the baseline under the basket. The players assume the defensive stance position, and everyone has the same foot forward. On the command "Advance," the players execute the advance step by pushing off the back foot and sliding the front foot forward toward an imaginary ball handler. The hand that corresponds with the front foot is brought up in the air as the defender yells, "Hey." On the command "Retreat," the players push their front foot into the floor and simultaneously take a step backward with the rear foot. On the command "Swing step," the players lock the shoulder, throw the elbow, and pivot the body in the direction of the imaginary dribbler. They take two defensive slides without bringing their feet together. The players stop and are in position to repeat the drill, with the opposite foot as the lead foot. The drill is done daily and is usually repeated going up and back down the court two times.

Defensive Slides

Once the ball handler has begun his or her dribble, the defender must contain penetration by maintaining the ball-you-basket principle. This is accomplished by using the defensive slide. Many coaches describe the action of the defensive slide as the step-and-slide, but we agree with coaches such as Lute Olson of Arizona and Jerry Krause of Gonzaga who call the movement the "power-push step."

"The 'power leg' approach has been a great teaching aid to our staff," said Olson. "We will get our players in the defensive stance and indicate we are going to have them slide to their right. At that time we tell them that their left (or trail) leg is to provide the power for the move and that they are to simply lift the right foot slightly and push with the left (or power) leg in this situation. We will have them make a three-step slide at half speed and require that they yell, 'Push! Push! Push!' The power leg theory is very simple—the trail leg in any slide should be the power source rather than being dragged."

Key teaching points are:

- Keep the knees bent.
- Use the power-push step.
- Have the head positioned directly above the center of the feet to maintain balance.
- Do not allow the head to bob up and down.
- Keep the feet apart. Do not bring the feet together during the defensive slide.
- Keep the hands active.

On-the-Ball Defensive Drills

Breakdown drills are essential for team defensive success. We use a series of drills that prepare defenders for guarding a ball handler. These drills emphasize stance, footwork, slides, foot quickness, and hand quickness.

One-on-One Drills

1. **One-on-One—Three Spots.** Three pairs of players are positioned at three spots on the midcourt line. (See Diagram 4.2.) The drill

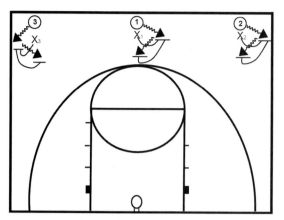

Diagram 4.2 One-on-One—Three Spots

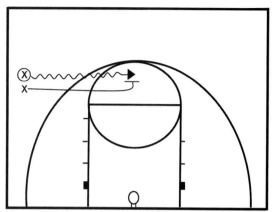

Diagram 4.3 Stopping Penetration at the Point

begins with O_1 trying to score against X_1. O_1 can go anywhere on the court but cannot turn his or her back to the defender. When the one-on-one action ends for this pair, O_2 tries to score against X_2. They will be followed by O_3 and X_3. The players switch between offense and defense and rotate to all three spots on the floor.

2. Stopping Penetration at the Point. The ball handler and defender are positioned at half-court adjacent to the sideline. The ball handler initiates the drill by dribbling toward the middle of the floor. (See Diagram 4.3.) The dribbler cannot make any countermove until he or she reaches the top of the circle. At this point, the ball handler can use any offensive move in an attempt to score. The defender's job is to stop the offensive player from turning the corner toward the basket. All shots must be contested and no second shots allowed.

3. Stopping Penetration in the Corner. The ball handler is positioned adjacent to the sideline and initiates the drill by dribbling toward the corner. (See Diagram 4.4.) The defender is trying to control the ball handler and then cut off the dribbler at approximately the 12-foot spot on the baseline. The dribbler is trying to turn the corner but can use any offensive move to the basket after he or she has been cut off.

Diagram 4.4 Stopping Penatration in the Corner

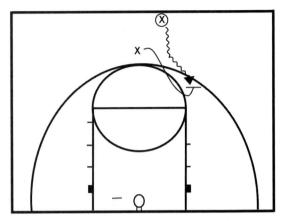

Diagram 4.5 Meeting the Dribbler at the Point

4. Meeting the Dribbler at the Point. The defender is waiting for the dribbler, who is driving quickly toward the free throw lane. (See Diagram 4.5.) The defensive player must contain penetration and at the same time not give up the uncontested jump shot.

5. Containing the Sideline Dribbler. The ball handler is positioned initially out-of-bounds and attempts to drive past the defender. The defensive player attempts to turn the dribbler and stop his or her penetration. (See Diagram 4.6.) Most offensive teams attack a zone by trying to penetrate the seams of the defense. The drill provides practice in containing this move. Use different starting points such as the wing and the corner.

6. One-on-One—Two Dribbles. This drill limits the offensive player to two dribbles. The ball handler is located approximately 18 feet from the basket at the point, wing, or corner. The defensive player must stop penetration, contest the shot, block out, and secure the rebound.

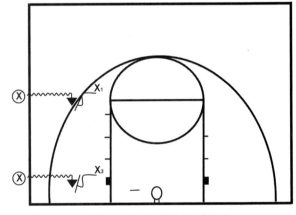

Diagram 4.6 Containing the Sideline Dribbler

5

Zone Defensive Principles

Zone defenses differ from man-to-man defenses in that players are assigned a particular area of the court to defend rather than a specific offensive player. A zone defender guards any offensive player that enters his or her area. For this reason, a zone defense would best be described as a combination defense because it merges zone principles with man-to-man principles.

One advantage of the zone defense is that it allows coaches to position their players exactly where they want them, regardless of where the offense places its players. This defensive strategy can be accomplished by placing the defensive players in a variety of different alignments. The name of the zone defense is determined by the player alignment. For example, the 3-2 zone has three players positioned on top of the defense and two defenders located on the back line as compared to the 2-3 zone, which has two defenders positioned on top and three defensive players on the back line.

Zone defenses are often referred to as even-front zones, such as the 2-3 and the 2-1-2, and odd-front zones, such as the 1-3-1, the 3-2, and the 1-2-2. The most important consideration regarding even-front and odd-front zone defenses is that differences among the various alignments occur only when the ball is at the point or in the midcourt area. Once the offensive team clearly establishes the ball on one side of the court, all zone defenses are alike in principle. Different alignments may require different defenders to cover the various court positions after the initial pass, but the areas to be covered remain the same.

Core Principles

No matter what zone defense a coach may select, there are 10 principles that must be adhered to in order for the defense to succeed. A short discussion of these principles follows.

1. *Zone Defense Is Hard Work.* Some coaches mistakenly believe that a zone defense is the easiest way to play defense. Nothing could be further from the truth! Successful zone defenses are comprised of defenders who crowd the ball handler, keep the ball out of the post area, contest shooters, block out, and aggressively rebound.
2. *Face the Ball.* Zone defensive players must turn their bodies so they are facing the ball. Remember, the only way an offensive team can score points is to put the ball in the basket. The ball is the most important thing on the court, and zone defenders must always see the ball and have their bodies positioned accordingly.
3. *Move When the Ball Moves.* Every defensive player must adjust his or her floor position on every ball movement. It is

mandatory that all players shift quickly. Two points of emphasis for zone defenders are to deny passes into the lane and to block the path of offensive cutters.

4. *Keep the Ball Out of the Red Zone.* This principle was discussed in Chapter 4 and it cannot be emphasized enough. The most dangerous areas on the floor are the elbows and the boxes. Zone defensive success depends on keeping the ball out of the red zone.

5. *Make the Offense Pass Around the Perimeter of the Zone.* Outstanding zone defenses do not allow the ball to penetrate the interior of the zone either by passing or dribbling. When opponents pass the ball, it should be around the perimeter of the zone rather than through it. An important teaching point for players to remember is that passes should be made in front of the zone defense, not inside the zone. If a ball is passed to a post player, it must be a lob pass rather than a direct pass.

6. *Talk.* All five defensive players must communicate with one another during the entire defensive possession. The defender on the ball handler must call out "Ball!" so that his or her teammates can make the proper adjustment. Back-line defensive players should always be communicating to their teammates. Legendary coach Don Meyer, who has won over 850 collegiate basketball games, named his match-up zone the "point and talk defense" because players are continually pointing to their offensive men and talking with their teammates.

7. *Anticipate.* Anticipation is essential. We like to use the phrases "play defense in advance" and "think one pass ahead." Every defender must know the offensive player he or she is responsible for. To do this correctly, it is important that defenders see both the ball and potential receivers. They must also keep their knees bent and be ready to move when the ball is passed or dribbled. Jerry Krause at Gonzaga uses the expression "know your next" to reinforce the concept of anticipation and assist defenders in identifying which offensive player will be their next responsibility if the ball is passed.

8. *Adjust.* Zone defenders must be ready to adjust at any time. It is impossible to prepare for every offensive tactic that an opponent may use. There will be times during a game that a defensive unit must alter their defense in order to stop an opponent's mode of attack. Jud Heathcote, who master-minded a 2-3 zone that led Michigan State to the 1979 National Championship, believed one of the key compo-nents in his zone was teaching players how to react to the offense and make the necessary adjustments. Heathcote told his players that their success as a defensive unit was depen-dent on their ability to "adjust." The coaching staff at Gonzaga University uses the phrase "figure it out" with their players to highlight the importance of making adjustments in the defensive scheme in order to stop the offense.

9. *Collective Responsibility.* The key to zone defensive success is collective responsibility. All five defenders must work to-gether as a single unit and make their shifts in complete uni-son. A defense is only as strong as its weakest link. Every team member must take pride in his or her defense and play the role that is needed. Successful zone defenses are the hall-mark of teamwork. Mike Krzyzewski illustrates the concept of collective responsibility by comparing each of five defen-sive players to a finger on a hand. Any one individually is important. But for the hand to be powerful, those five fin-gers must come together and form a fist. Thus, a team will not become a strong defensive unit until any combination of five players can play as one.

10. *Don't Beat Yourself.* The basic premise in basketball is, don't beat yourself. When playing a zone defense, it is essential to position your players in the areas of the court where your opponent is the strongest. If your opponent's inside game is superior, it is critical to align your defenders so the opposing offense cannot control that area. Give them only the lowest percentage perimeter shot and force them to beat you from the outside.

6

3-2 Zone Defense

The 3-2 zone was originally designed to stop out-side shooters by placing the strength of the defense above the free throw line. At the time of its creation, zone defenses were considered stationary, and there was very little movement by the defensive players. Today, that is not the case. In order for the 3-2 zone to be effective, individual man-to-man defense must be taught both on and off the ball.

Basketball experts, such as Bob Knight and Lute Olson, have recognized coauthor Casey as one of the foremost zone coaches in the world. The 3-2 zone defensive slides are the precursor to success in all zone defenses.

Initial Alignment and Player Characteristics

The initial alignment for the 3-2 zone defense is shown in Diagram 6.1. With the advent of the three-point line, the point defender's floor position was moved to the top of the circle so it resembles a 1-2-2 zone. The point defender is designated in the diagrams as X_1, the wing defenders are X_2 and X_3, and the back-line defenders are X_4 and X_5.

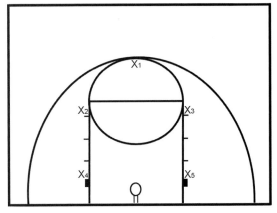

Diagram 6.1 Initial Alignment

Point Defender—X_1

The point defender, X_1, is positioned at the top of the circle unless pressing tactics are being employed. Desirable characteristics for X_1 are:

- Lateral quickness
- Active hands
- Excellent anticipator
- Able to keep the ball out of the high post area
- Best ball handler for the fast break

Wing Defender—X_2

The defensive player X_2, is the left wing. The inside foot of X_2 should be at the junction between the foul line and the free throw lane. This area is called the "elbow." Desirable characteristics for X_2 are:

- Best wing defender, since most teams initiate their offense on the right side

- Aggressive rebounder
- Better ball handler of the wings
- Agile and able to move out quickly on the fast break

Wing Defender—X_3

The defensive player, X_3, is the right wing. The inside foot of X_3 should be at the junction between the foul line and the free throw lane. Desirable characteristics for X_3 are:

- Best wing rebounder
- Loves physical contact and rebounding
- Key defensive player
- Agile and able to move out quickly on the fast break

Back-Line Defender—X_4

The back-line defender on the left side is X_4. The rule for this defender is to straddle the lane above the block as high (away from the basket) as the offense allows. Desirable characteristics for X_4 are:

- Quickest of the back-line defenders because he or she will be pulled out to the corner more than X_5
- Able to rebound against an opponent's post player
- Better athlete of the two back-line players
- Able to fill the lane on the fast break or be the trailer

Back-Line Defender—X_5

The back-line defender on the right side is X_5. The rule for this defender's initial position is identical to X_4. Desirable characteristics for X_5 are:

- Tallest and strongest of the back-line defenders
- Able to defend the post area and be an enforcer

- Hard worker who has a passion for contact inside the lane
- Physically tough
- Able to cover the corner without curtailing rebounding

Areas of Responsibility

Defensive players are responsible for the ball in their designated area.

They must become experts in sliding to the correct spot on the court depending on the location of the ball and the positioning of the opponents. There must be constant communication between defenders so there is no confusion of assignments. Diagram 6.2 illustrates the general areas of responsibilities.

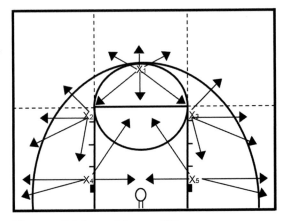

Diagram 6.2 Areas of Responsibility

A key point that must continually be emphasized is that successful coaches adjust the slides based on the strengths and weaknesses of their players and the opponents. We are providing the starting point for the 3-2 zone and encourage coaches to be creative and develop slides that maximize the strengths of their players and hide their deficiencies.

3-2 Zone Slides

A synchronized effort among the point defenders, wing defenders, and the back-line defenders is paramount to defensive success. Using the whole method of teaching, the defenders learn their basic slides and individual responsibilities playing against five offensive players, and then a sixth player is added. The offensive players stay relatively stationary and are located in the following spots: point, high post, wings, and corners.

Ball at the Point

Diagram 6.3 shows the floor position of the defensive players when the ball is at the point.

- The point defender, X_1, picks up the ball handler and defends against the three-point shot, dribble penetration, and the pass into the high post. It is important for X_1 not to go out too far past the top of the circle because it is his or her responsibility to keep the ball out of the

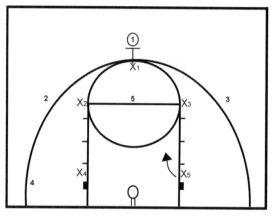

Diagram 6.3 Ball at the Point

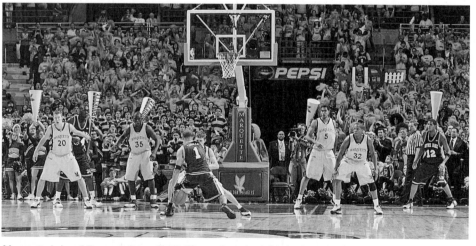

Marquette is in a 3-2 zone defense. Travis Diener, the point defender, is pressuring the ball handler. The wing defenders, Steve Novak (#20) and Joe Chapman (#32), are positioned at the elbow and are facing the ball. The back-line defenders, Marcus Jackson (#35) and Scott Merritt (#5), are located above the block and are straddling the lane line.

high post. Overextending leaves the high post area less protected.

- The wing defenders, X_2 and X_3, line up on the free throw line
extended with their inside foot on the free throw line to prevent the ball from being passed to the high post. This position
is called "hold at the elbow." X_2 and X_3 must anticipate the
ball being passed from the point to the wing and be ready to
quickly slide out and defend against the three-point shot and
dribble penetration.

- The position of the back-line defenders, X_4 and X_5, is critical.
When there is an offensive player in the high post, one of the
back-line defensive players must be in the "up position." The
"up-defender" cheats up a few steps so that he or she can defend the high post in case the ball is passed into this position.
The up-defender may be preassigned by the coach, or it could
be determined by the floor position of the ball.

- In Diagram 6.3, X_5 slides into the up position. X_4 straddles
the lane and is positioned above the block.

Pass from the Point to the Wing

Diagram 6.4 illustrates the defensive slides when the ball is passed
from the point (1) to the wing (3).

- X_1 quickly slides to the elbow and prevents a pass to a high
post. This area is called the "red zone" and was discussed in
Chapters 4 and 5. Defensive success depends on keeping the
ball out of the red zone.

- X_3 slides out and defends against the three-point shot. The
teaching phrase used when defending the ball handler is
"crowd the ball." X_3 employs man-to-man defensive principles
and maintains a floor position between the ball and the basket
(buttocks-to-basket rule) to prevent dribble penetration into
the middle. If the offensive wing (3) attempts to dribble, X_3
makes sure that he or she dribbles in an arc rather than a
straight-line drive to the basket.

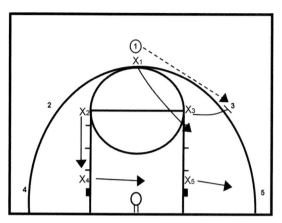

Diagram 6.4 Pass from the Point to the Wing

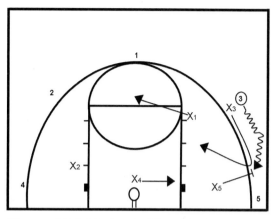

Diagram 6.5 Dribble from the Wing to the Corner

- X_5 slides to a floor position halfway between the corner and the lane and anticipates a pass from the wing to the corner. This position is called the "cheat position" because it shortens the distance that X_5 must travel in order to cover the corner.
- X_4 moves to the middle of the lane in front of the basket and protects the lane area.
- X_2 drops and has the responsibility of defending the lob pass or the crosscourt pass to either 2 or 4. X_2 has one foot in the lane and faces the ball at all times. X_2's position is called the "drop position." As a point of reference for the depth of the drop, X_2 should be on an imaginary line drawn between the ball handler (3) and the weak side corner.

Dribble from the Wing to the Corner

Diagram 6.5 shows the defensive slides when the wing (3) dribbles toward the corner player (5).

- When the offensive wing (3) dribbles to the corner, X_3 releases the dribbler to the back-line defender, X_5. The verbal command is "Switch!" It is important not to have two defenders guarding one offensive player.

- The location of the switch can vary but it is generally 3 to 4 feet below the free throw line extended. It is better for the back-line defender to be late rather than early so that the back line is not overexposed.
- X_3 protects the side post area.
- X_1 defends against the diagonal crosscourt pass.
- X_2 defends against a crosscourt pass to either 2 or 4.

Pass from the Wing to the Corner

When the ball is passed from the wing (3) to the corner (5), there are two defensive options for the strong side-wing defender. One is called "blocking the lane" and the other is called "plugging the middle." Factors such as the opponent's scouting report, time remaining, and score of the game dictate the best option.

Diagram 6.6 illustrates the defensive slides when X_3 blocks the lane.

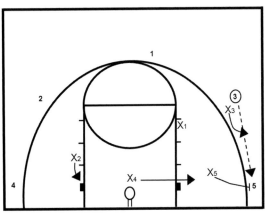

Diagram 6.6 Pass from the Wing to the Corner (Blocking the Lane)

- X_5 quickly closes out against 5 and defends against the perimeter shot and drive.
- X_4 slides over in front of any offensive low post player and always faces the ball. Depending on the scouting report, there may be some post players that are better to play behind.
- X_1 faces the ball and takes away any direct high post diagonal pass.
- X_2 drops to a weak side rebounding position.
- X_3 slides into the passing lane and denies the pass back to the wing. This position is called "blocking the lane." It stops ball

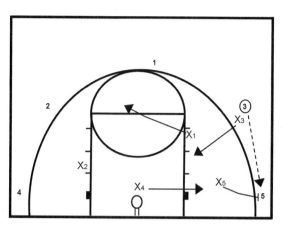

Diagram 6.7 Pass from the Wing to the Corner (Plugging the Middle)

reversal and keeps the ball out of the hands of an excellent three-point shooter from the wing. X_3 faces the ball handler with the arms extended. The only pass that could be made back to 3 would be a lob pass.

Diagram 6.7 illustrates the defensive slides when using the strategy called "plugging the middle." It works best against teams with strong post players or poor perimeter shooters. The only defenders whose responsibilities change are X_3 and X_1.

- X_3 collapses and keeps the ball out of the side-post area. This position is called "plugging the middle."
- The depth of X_3's drop depends on the scouting report. It must be noted that X_3 must be prepared to slide back out to the wing quickly if a pass is thrown from 5 to 3, especially if 3 is an excellent perimeter shooter.
- When X_3 plugs the middle, X_1 adjusts his or her position and defends against the cross-court diagonal pass. X_1 moves to a spot somewhere between the free throw line and the top of the circle.

When the ball is in the corner and the defensive coverage is plugging the middle, defenders X_1, X_2, X_3, and X_4 are in an alignment that resembles a box. (See Diagram 6.8.) This is called the "box move."

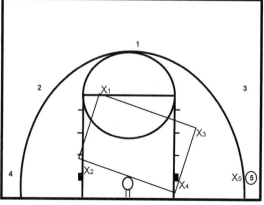

Diagram 6.8 The Box Move

Steve Novak (#20) "plugs the middle" and is prepared to intercept the pass into the low post area.

Dribble from the Corner to the Wing

Diagram 6.9 illustrates the defensive slides when the corner (5) dribbles toward the wing.

- The wing defender (X_3) quickly moves into position as if to double-team the dribbler (5).
- The back-line defender (X_5) stays with 5 until X_3 picks up the ball. At that time, X_5 drops to back into the cheat position, which is a floor position halfway between the corner and the free throw lane.

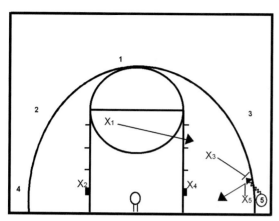

Diagram 6.9 Dribble from the Corner to the Wing

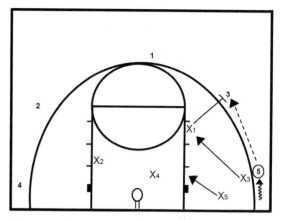

Diagram 6.10 Pass to the Wing (Off the Dribble)

- X_4 guards the strong side low post area.
- X_2 has the weak side rebounding area.
- X_1 slides across the lane and defends the elbow area.

Diagram 6.10 shows the defensive coverage if 5 throws a quick pass to the wing (3) off the dribble.

- X_1 slides from the elbow to the wing and defends against the three-point shot and the drive. This is necessary because it would be very difficult for X_3 to get to the wing quickly enough to stop 3's perimeter shot.
- X_3 moves up to protect the elbow area.
- X_5 defends the low post area.
- X_4 is in the lane in front of the basket.
- X_2 is prepared to cover the next pass made to the weak side of the floor.

Pass from the Corner to the Wing

Diagram 6.11 illustrates the defensive coverage when the ball is passed from the corner (5) to the wing (3).

- X_3 slides out to defend 3 and stop both the perimeter shot and the drive.
- X_1 guards the elbow area.
- X_4 moves in front of the basket in the lane.
- X_5 returns to the halfway corner position (cheat position).
- X_2 slides up to approximately the level of the ball or slightly below.

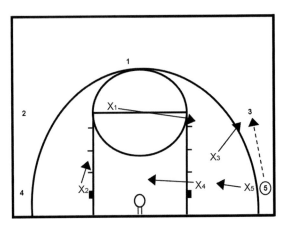

Diagram 6.11 Pass from the Corner to the Wing

Pass from the Wing to the Point

Diagram 6.12 shows the defensive coverage when the ball is passed from the wing (3) to the point (1).

- X_1 slides to the outside shoulder of 1 in order to prevent the quick dribble split.
- X_3 moves quickly to the elbow and prevents a gap in the defense.
- X_2 travels up the lane to the elbow.
- X_4 straddles the free throw lane line and is positioned above the box.
- X_5 slides into the up position because 4 is in the high post.

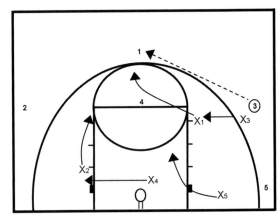

Diagram 6.12 Pass from the Wing to the Point

Pass from the Point to the High Post

When the ball is passed to the high post from the point, X_1 can either double-team the post player or "shadow" the high post and be ready to defend the kick-back pass to 1.

Diagram 6.13 illustrates the defensive slides when X_1 double-teams the high post.

- X_5 quickly moves up to defend the high post (4). X_5 was anticipating the pass from the point to the high post and was in the up position.
- X_4 moves across the lane into the "tandem position." X_4's responsibility is identi-cal to that of the back-line defender in a 3-on-2 fast-break situation. If 4 passes to the wing, X_4 moves to the strong side.

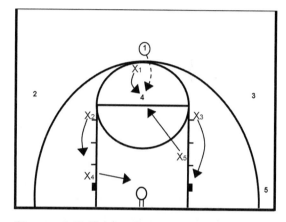

Diagram 6.13 High Post Coverage (Double-Team)

- X_1 turns and double-teams the high post with X_5.
- The wing defenders, X_2 and X_3, drop back to protect against the baseline pass. The level of drop is approximately a 45-degree angle in relation to the high post. X_2 and X_3 will cover the next pass on their respective side of the court whether it is at the wing or the corner.

When the ball is thrown into the high post and 1 is an outstanding perimeter shooter, X_1 does not double-team the high post because X_1 would not be able to get back and defend the three-point shot. Diagram 6.14 shows the defensive coverage when using the shadow technique.

- X_5 quickly moves up and defends the high post (4).
- X_4 moves to the center of the lane into the tandem position.
- X_1 shadows the high post and is ready to defend the kick-back pass to 1.
- The wing defenders, X_2 and X_3, drop back to protect against the baseline pass.

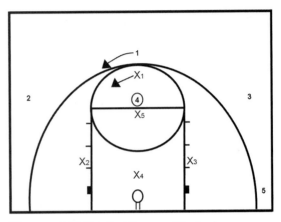

Diagram 6.14 High Post Coverage (Shadow)

Pass from the High Post to the Wing

Diagram 6.15 shows the defensive slides when the high post (4) passes the ball to the wing (2).

- X_2 slides out and crowds the ball handler.
- X_4 moves to the cheat position, which is halfway between the corner and the free throw lane.
- X_5 drops into the lane in front of the basket.
- X_1 moves to the elbow and defends against a pass into the high post area.

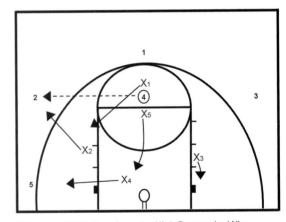

Diagram 6.15 Pass from the High Post to the Wing

- X_3 slides to the drop position and protects against either the lob pass or the crosscourt pass.

Pass from the High Post to the Corner

Diagram 6.16 illustrates the defensive coverage when the high post
(4) passes the ball to the corner (5).

- X_3 slides out quickly to
  temporarily prevent a shot
  or a drive until X_4 can take
  his or her spot.
- X_4 moves across the lane
  protecting the low post
  and box and continues out
  to the corner and picks up
  the ball handler. This
  releases X_3 to move to the
  free throw lane.
- X_5 initially drops into the
  lane in front of the basket.
  As X_4 moves to the corner,
  X_5 slides in front of the box.
- X_2 drops back into the weak side rebounding position.
- X_1 initially moves to the elbow and then reacts to X_3's slide
  by moving over to protect against the diagonal pass. The
  defenders are now in the box move that was illustrated in
  Diagram 6.8 on page 91.

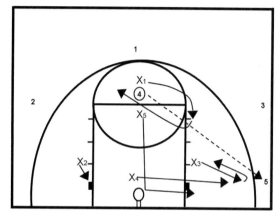

Diagram 6.16 Pass from the High Post to the Corner

Pass from the Wing to the Side Post

Diagram 6.17 shows the defensive coverage when the ball is passed from the wing (3) to the side post (4).

- X_4 moves up and defends the side post. This is called the "up man rule," which means the back-line defender opposite the ball always moves up to cover the post.
- X_5 slides to the lane and protects against a high-low pass.
- X_1 does not double-team the ball. Instead, X_1 goes to the opposite elbow.

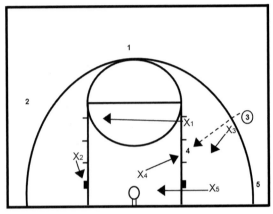

Diagram 6.17 Pass from the Wing to the Side Post

- X_3 drops either to the level of the ball or slightly below and protects the baseline. X_3 is prepared to cover the first pass to his or her side.
- X_2 drops to the block and protects against a pass into the lane. X_2 is also responsible for a pass to either 4 or 2.

Pass from the Side Post to the Weak Side Wing

Diagram 6.18 illustrates the defensive slides when the ball is passed from the side post (4) to the weak side wing (2).

- X_2 slides out and covers the ball handler.
- X_5 moves to the cheat position.
- X_4 slides in front of the basket.
- X_1 covers the strong side elbow.
- X_3 moves to the drop position and defends against the lob pass or the crosscourt pass.

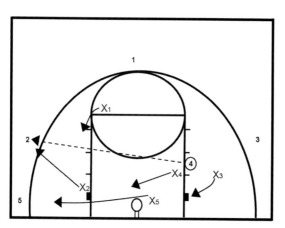

Diagram 6.18 Pass from the Side Post to the Weak Side Wing

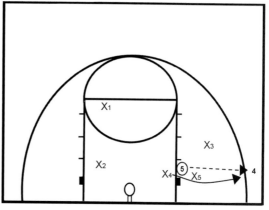

Diagram 6.19 Pass from the Low Post to the Corner (Option #1)

Pass from the Low Post to the Corner

When the ball is passed from a double-team in the low post to the corner, there are two ways to cover this situation.

Diagram 6.19 shows the first option.

- X_4 loops around the low post (5) and guards the ball in the corner.
- X_5 stays and fronts the low post.

Diagram 6.20 illustrates the second option.

- X_5 slides out and defends the ball in the corner.
- X_4 must then fight through and get in front of the low post player.

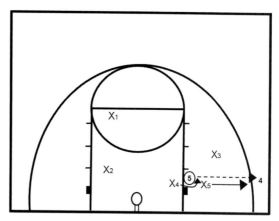

Diagram 6.20 Pass from the Low Post to the Corner (Option #2)

Rebound Positions

When a shot is taken, the phrase "elbows, boxes, and middle of the lane" prevails. It is important to treat every shot as if it were a pass into the post. The back-line defender opposite the shot must step into the middle of the lane, and the other defenders must fill the boxes and the elbows.

Most critics of the zone defense believe that it does not provide the necessary rebounding coverage. The authors strongly disagree. A zone defense does provide excellent rebounding coverage as long as the elbows, boxes, and middle of the lane are filled on every shot attempt. Eliminating second shots is crucial to team success. Every defender must be an aggressive rebounder. There can be no spectators. Every player must get in the action.

Coaches determine the rebounding nature of their teams. They must hold players accountable and inspire them to take pride in limiting opponents to one shot. Blocking out and rebounding must be stressed every day. Former coach Tynes Hildebrand at Northwestern State University had one of the best rebounding teams in the country because he assigned one assistant coach to enforce his rebounding rules during every drill in practice.

The rebounding coverage discussed in the following sections is only a guideline. Coaches should make adjustments according to the strengths and weaknesses of their players.

Shot from the Point

Diagram 6.21 shows the rebounding responsibilities when the shot is taken from the point.

- X_1 blocks out the shooter and then moves to the elbow on the side of the up-defender.
- X_3 is responsible for the box area on the side of the up-defender.

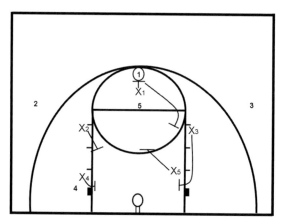

Diagram 6.21 Shot from the Point

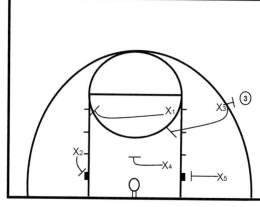

Diagram 6.22 Shot from the Wing

- X_2 rebounds the elbow area on his or her side.
- X_4 rebounds the block area on his or her side of the court.
- X_5 is responsible for the middle-of-the-lane rebounding area.

Shot from the Wing

Diagram 6.22 illustrates the rebounding responsibilities when the shot is taken from the wing.

- X_3 blocks out the shooter and then moves to the elbow.
- X_1 moves across the lane to the far elbow and looks to block out any weak side perimeter player crashing the boards. X_1 must be aggressive and not allow a back-side rebounder a clear path to the boards.
- X_5 blocks out any opponent in the vicinity of the strong side box.
- X_4 has the middle-of-the-lane rebounding responsibilities.
- X_2 rebounds the weak side box area.

Shot from the Corner

Diagram 6.23 illustrates the rebounding coverage when the shot is taken from the corner.

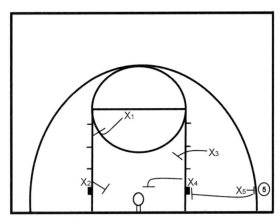

Diagram 6.23 Shot from the Corner

- X_5 blocks out the shooter and proceeds to the box area.
- X_2 moves to the weak side box.
- X_1 has rebounding responsibilities at the weak side elbow.
- X_3 rebounds the strong side box area.
- X_4 must initially be conscious of the strong side box area, but his or her prime area of responsibility is the middle of the lane.

3-2 Zone Breakdown Drills

After teaching the unit slides and rebounding responsibilities of the 3-2 zone, the next step is to incorporate breakdown drills for the front-line and back-line defenders. It is easy to break down into halves of the court with the three front-line defenders working against six passers at one end, and two back-line defenders working against six passers at the other end. Have each group of defenders work for 30 seconds, and then have another group come in. The best way to become an outstanding zone defensive team is to work on these breakdown drills the entire season.

Front-Line Drill—6 vs. 3

In this drill, the front-line defenders respond to ball movement. The six offensive players are located at the point, wings, and corners. They must stand relatively stationary.

Initial Position—Ball at Point. The drill begins with the ball at the point as shown in Diagram 6.24.

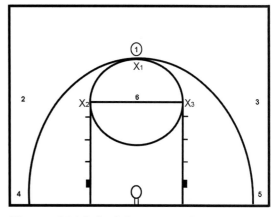

Diagram 6.24 Ball at Point

- X_1 defends against the perimeter shot, dribble penetration, and the pass into the high post.
- X_2 and X_3 are in the hold-at-the-elbow positions. The inside foot of X_2 and X_3 is placed at the junction of the free throw lane line and the free throw line to prevent the ball from being passed into the high post.
- X_2 and X_3 must anticipate the ball being passed to the wing and be ready to quickly move and defend the wing player.

Pass from the Point to the Wing and Then to the Corner. The ball is passed from the point (1) to the wing (2) and then passed to the corner (4). On the pass from 1 to 2 (see Diagram 6.25):

- X_1 quickly slides to the elbow area and covers the high post area.
- X_2 slides out and crowds the wing (2). X_2 prevents both the outside shot and dribble penetration.

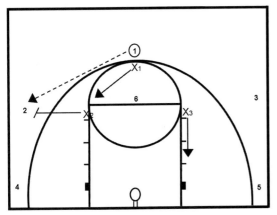

Diagram 6.25 Pass from the Point to the Wing

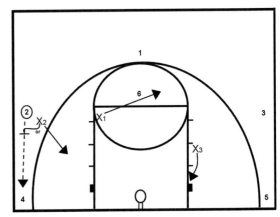

Diagram 6.26 Pass from the Wing to the Corner

- X_3 is in the drop position and has the responsibility of defending the lob pass or the crosscourt pass. X_3 should have one foot in the lane and face the ball.

When the ball is passed from the wing (2) to the corner (4) (see Diagram 6.26):

- X_1 moves to a spot between the free throw line and the top of the circle and protects against the diagonal pass.
- X_3 drops low and is positioned for the weak side rebound.
- Depending on the scouting report, X_2 can either block the lane (deny the pass back to the wing) or plug the middle (provide inside help). Both slides were explained earlier in this chapter.

Skip Pass from the Corner to the Point and then to the Wing. The ball is passed from the corner (4) to the point (1) and then passed to the wing (3). On the pass from 4 to 1(see Diagram 6.27):

- X_2 moves from the box-move position to the hold-at-the-elbows position.

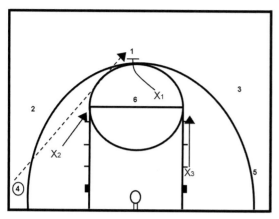

Diagram 6.27 Skip Pass from the Corner to the Point

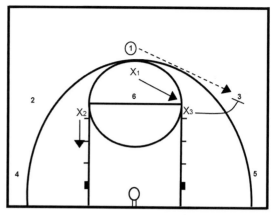

Diagram 6.28 Pass from the Point to the Wing

- X_3 slides up the lane to the hold-at-the-elbow position.
- X_1 crowds the ball handler by sliding to 1's opposite shoulder. X_1 prevents the perimeter shot and dribble penetration.

When the ball is passed from the point (1) to the wing (3) (see Diagram 6.28):

- X_3 slides out and crowds the ball.
- X_1 slides to the elbow area and prevents a pass into the high post.
- X_2 is in the drop position and has the responsibility of defending the lob pass or the crosscourt pass. X_2 should have one foot in the lane and face the ball.

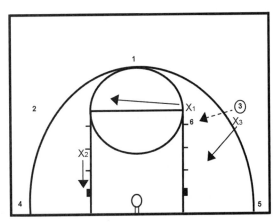

Diagram 6.29 Pass from the Wing to the Elbow

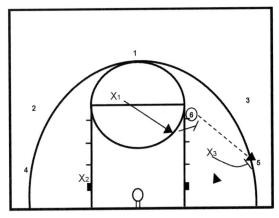

Diagram 6.30 Pass from the Elbow to the Corner

Pass from the Wing to the Elbow and Then to the Corner. The ball is passed from the wing (3) to the post player (6) and then passed to the wing (3). On the pass from 3 to 6 (see Diagram 6.29):

- X_3 drops below the level of the ball, protecting the pass to the baseline.
- X_1 moves opposite to protect against a diagonal pass.
- X_2 drops to the weak side box.

When the ball is passed from the elbow (6) to the corner (5) (see Diagram 6.30):

- X_3 defends 5 (Note: X_3 will remain on 5 until the ball is passed out of the corner, then will return to his or her normal zone slides).
- X_1 quickly shifts back to the strong side and defends the side post area.
- X_2 remains at the weak side box.

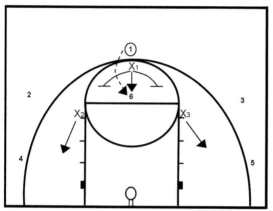

Diagram 6.31 Pass from the Point to the High Post

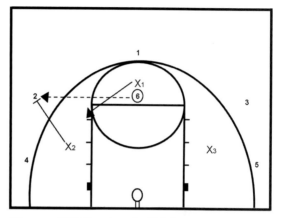

Diagram 6.32 Pass from the High Post to the Wing

Pass from the Point to the High Post. As illustrated in Diagram 6.31, the ball is passed from the point (1) to the high post (6). On the pass from 1 to 6:

- X_1 either turns and double-teams the ball or shadows the high post. The shadow technique allows for a quicker recovery on an excellent shooting point guard.
- X_2 and X_3 drop back and defend against a pass to the baseline. They will take the first pass to their respective side of the court.

Pass from the High Post to the Wing and Then a Crosscourt Pass to the Wing. The high post (6) passes to the wing (2), and then the ball is passed crosscourt to 3.

On the pass from 6 to 2 (see Diagram 6.32):

- X_2 slides up to defend 2.
- X_1 drops to the elbow area protecting against a pass into the high post.
- X_3 remains in the drop position and defends against the lob pass or the crosscourt pass.

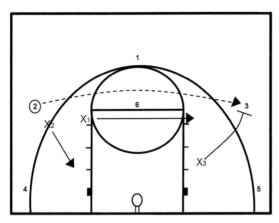

Diagram 6.33 Crosscourt Pass (Wing to Wing)

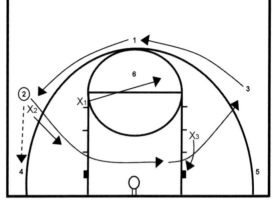

Diagram 6.34 Defending the Wing Cutter

When the ball is passed from 2 to (see Diagram 6.33):

- X_3 slides up to defend 3.
- X_1 shifts quickly across the lane to the strong side elbow area.
- X_2 moves to the drop position and defends against the lob pass or the crosscourt pass.

Defending the Wing Cutter. As illustrated in Diagram 6.34, the wing (2) passes to the corner (4) and cuts through. 1 replaces 2 at the wing, and 3 replaces 1 at the point. To defend against a wing cutter:

- X_2 honors the cutter for three or four steps and stops a direct pass back to 2. X_2 surveys the situation and can either plug the middle or defend the wing position if it is filled.
- X_3 drops to the weak side box.
- X_1 must read X_2 and adjust accordingly. If X_2 plugs the middle, X_1 moves away to defend against a diagonal pass. If X_2 slides out to defend the wing, X_1 guards the elbow area.

Back-Line Drill—6 vs. 2

In this drill, the two back-line defenders respond to ball movement. The six offensive players are located at the point, wings, corners and high post must remain in their respective areas.

Initial Position—Ball at the Point. The drill begins with the ball at the point as shown in Diagram 6.35.

- X_4 straddles the lane and is positioned above the block.
- X_5 is in the up position and is ready to defend the high post if necessary.

Pass from the Point to the Wing and Then to the Corner. The ball is thrown from the point (1) to the wing (2), and then passed to the corner (4). On the pass from 1 to 2 (see Diagram 6.36):

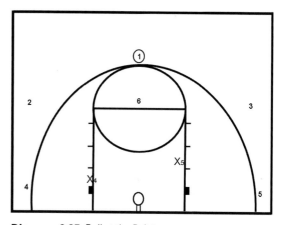

Diagram 6.35 Ball at the Point

- X_4 slides to the cheat position, which is a floor position halfway between the corner and the free throw lane.
- X_5 shifts into the lane. X_5's position will be determined by the scouting report. It may be directly in front of the basket or adjusted slightly due to the strength of the opponent's inside game.

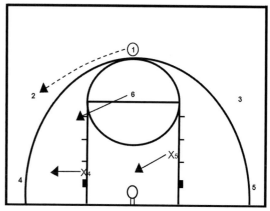

Diagram 6.36 Pass from the Point to the Wing

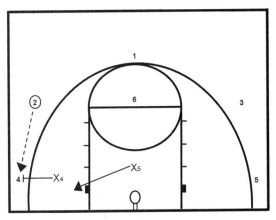

Diagram 6.37 Pass from the Wing to the Corner

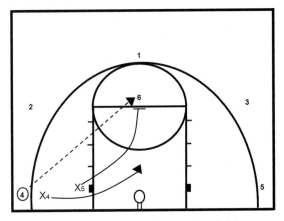

Diagram 6.38 Pass from the Corner to the High Post

When the ball is passed from 2 to 4 (see Diagram 6.37):

- X_4 slides out and defends 4 using the team's man-to-man defensive principles.
- X_5 moves in front of the box.

Pass from the Corner to the High Post and Then to the Opposite Corner. The ball is passed from the corner (4) to the high post (6) and then to the opposite corner (5). On the pass from 4 to 6 (see Diagram 6.38):

- X_5 slides up to defend 6.
- X_4 moves to the center of the lane and is the back-line defender in the tandem position with X_5.

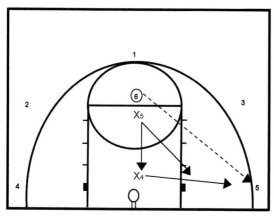

Diagram 6.39 Pass from the High Post to the Corner

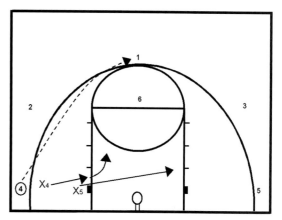

Diagram 6.40 Pass from the Corner to the Point

When the ball is passed from 6 to 5 (see Diagram 6.39):

- X_4 slides out to the corner and defends 5.
- X_5 drops down either to the box or to the middle of the lane.

Pass from the Corner to the Point and Then to the High Post. The ball is passed from the corner (4) to the point (1) and then to the high post (6). On the pass from 4 to 1 (see Diagram 6.40):

- X_4 and X_5 move into their positions when the ball is at the point. This is called "going back home."
- X_4 slides to the up position.

When the ball is passed from 1 to 6 (see Diagram 6.41):

- X_4 moves up and defends 6.
- X_5 slides into the lane and defends the low post.

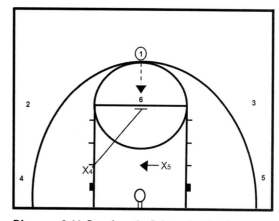

Diagram 6.41 Pass from the Point to the High Post

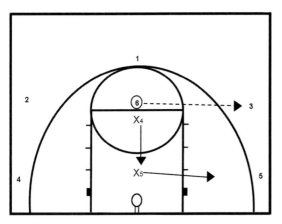

Diagram 6.42 Pass from the High Post to the Wing

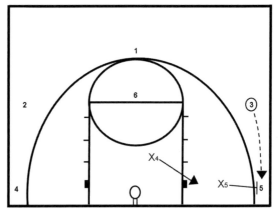

Diagram 6.43 Pass from the Wing to the Corner

Pass from the High Post to the Wing and Then to the Corner. The high post (6) passes to the wing (3), and then the ball is passed to 5 in the corner. On the pass from 6 to 3 (see Diagram 6.42):

- X_5 moves into the cheat position.
- X_4 drops back.

When the ball is passed from the wing (3) to the corner (5) (see Diagram 6.43):

- X_5 breaks out to the corner and defends 5.
- X_4 fronts the low post player.

The Whole Method of Learning

It is critical to practice the 3-2 zone with five defenders working together as one unit. We recommend initially working against five stationary offensive players who pass the ball but do not shoot.

Then add a sixth, seventh, and eighth offensive player so the defense can cover various situations. The offensive players simply move the ball and let the defenders work on their slides.

7

2-3 Zone Defense

In the 2-3 zone defense, three defenders are placed close to the basket so they can defend against post players and rebound missed shots. The slides in the 2-3 zone are very similar to the 3-2 zone defense, once the ball is at the wing. The 2-3 zone can either be an active or a passive defense depending on the score of the game, the time remaining, and the strengths and weaknesses of your opponent.

An important mentor for coauthor Casey was John Egli from Penn State University. Egli played and coached for John Lawther, who was the founder of the sliding zone defense. Lawther and Egli stressed that every time the ball was passed or dribbled, every defensive player automatically slid to a certain

The defenders quickly fall back into the 2-3 alignment. All the defenders' arms are out and their knees are bent.

position on the court relative to the location of the ball and the basket. Egli believed it was essential that defenders were alert, aggressive, and team-oriented. "The zone is a team defense and requires the utmost in teamwork," said Egli. "It will not work unless each player cooperates through talking and working together."

Initial Alignment and Player Characteristics

The initial alignment for the 2-3 zone defense is shown in Diagram 7.1.

Front-Line Defender—X_1

The defensive player, X_1, is the front-line defender on the left wing. X_1's initial position is parallel with X_2. Desirable characteristics for X_1 are:

- Lateral quickness and active hands
- Able to cover both the point and the wing
- Excellent anticipator
- Good at retrieving medium-range rebounds and loose balls
- Best ball handler for the fast break

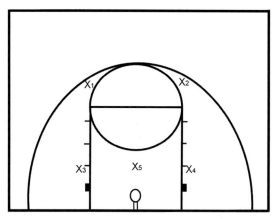

Diagram 7.1 Initial Alignment

Front-Line Defender—X₂

The defensive player, X_2, is the front-line defender on the right wing. X_2's initial position is parallel with X_1. Desirable characteristics for X_2 are:

- Lateral quickness and active hands
- Able to cover both the point and the wing
- Excellent anticipator
- Good at retrieving medium-range rebounds and loose balls
- Agile and able to move out quickly on the fast break

Back-Line Defender—X₃

The defensive player, X_3, is the back-line defender on the left side of the court. X_3's initial alignment should be with the first marker above the block. Desirable characteristics for this player are:

- Able to cover the wing quickly and then retreat back to the lane area
- Loves physical contact and rebounding
- Agile and able to defend against shots from the corner
- Able to move out quickly on the fast break

Back-Line Defender—X₄

The defensive player, X_4, is the back-line defender on the right side of the court and is positioned at the first marker above the block. The necessary characteristics for X_4 are:

- Able to cover the wing quickly and then retreat back to the lane area
- Physically tough
- Relentless in his or her attempts to retrieve missed shots
- Able to rebound against an opponent's post player
- Able to defend against shots from the corner
- Able to fill the lane on the fast break or be the trailer

Middle Defender—X₅

The middle defender is X_5. Desirable characteristics for X_5 are:

- Tallest and strongest of the back-line defenders
- Able to defend the post area and be an enforcer
- Strong rebounder
- Hard worker who has a passion for contact inside the lane
- Physically tough
- Good passer and is able to initiate the fast break with a quick outlet pass

Initial Pick-Up of the Ball

It is critical for one of the front-line defenders to pick up the ball at approximately the three-point line. This player is called the "up-defender" and guards the ball handler using man-to-man principles. The other front-line defender moves to the elbow area, approximately one step in front of the free throw line. This defensive player is called

the "back-defender." The positioning of the up- and back-de-
fenders is a counter against an
odd-player offensive front, such
as a 1-3-1 alignment. The position of the up- defender makes
the zone look more like a 1-2-2
zone rather than a 2-3 zone.

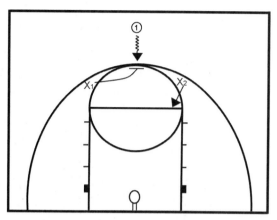

Diagram 7.2 Up-Defender and Backline-Defender

There are different ways that a
coach can determine which front-
line defender should be in the
up position. A coach can permanently assign a player to be the up-
defender, or it could be the defender positioned on the ball side.

Diagram 7.2 illustrates the up and back positioning of the front-line
defenders when X_1 defends the ball handler. X_2 drops to the elbow area
and is the back-defender.

Key Concepts in the 2-3 Zone Defense

A synchronized effort between the front-line, middle, and back-line
defenders is essential. It begins with one of the front-line defenders
picking up the ball handler and becoming the up-defender. This is
critical because it dictates the floor position for all the other defenders. Key concepts in the 2-3 zone defense are the cheat position, bump
down, X moves, high post coverage, and elbows and blocks rule.

Cheat Position

Both back-line defenders (X_3 and X_4) must become skilled in defending a wing and stopping the three-point shot. The best way to
do this is to take several steps toward the wing when the ball is at the
point. This floor position is called the "cheat position."

When #11 is the up-defender, #42 moves toward the wing into the "cheat position."

A back-line defender must read the front-line players to determine whether he or she should be in the cheat position. In Diagram 7.3, X_3 sees that the front-line defender on his or her side (X_1) is the up-defender. X_3 immediately gets into the cheat position. X_3 is now in position to defend the wing if the pass is made from 1 to 2. X_3's anticipation is critical because he or she must move the moment the ball leaves the hands of the passer (1).

In Diagram 7.4, X_4 sees that the front-line defender on his or her side is the up-defender and moves into the cheat position.

Bump Down

When the ball is passed from the point (1) to the wing (2), X_3, the back-line defender who was in the cheat position, slides out to "bother" 2 and stop a three-point shot. X_1 drops to the elbow momentarily and then quickly slides out to cover 3 and "crowd the ball." This initiates the "bump down move" between X_1 and X_3. This is not designed to be a trap. As X_1 arrives, X_3 releases. X_3 should drop back, face the ball, and be ready to cover a pass to the corner. (See Diagram 7.5.)

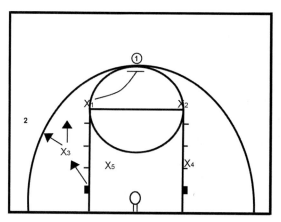

Diagram 7.3 Cheat Position (X$_3$)

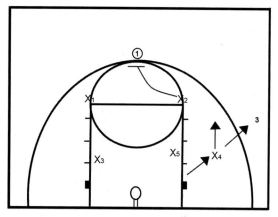

Diagram 7.4 Cheat Position (X$_4$)

X Moves

An alternative to covering the wing with the bump down is to use either the "deep X move" or the "shallow X move." These moves may initially appear too difficult or unsafe to implement, but they have been used with great success because most offensive teams do not immediately recognize how to exploit them.

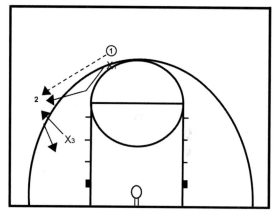

Diagram 7.5 Bump Down Move

Deep X Move. As shown in Diagram 7.6, X$_3$ steps out and defends the wing (2). There is no bump down. X$_1$ slides to the elbow. On the pass from 2 to 4, X$_3$ makes a diagonal cut to the weak side box. He or she now becomes the back-line defender on the weak side. X$_5$ slides to the corner and guards the ball. X$_4$ covers the low post area. X$_1$ has two options. He or she can either block the lane or plug the middle using the box move. Both options were discussed in Chapter 6.

Shallow X Move. As illustrated in Diagram 7.7, X$_3$ steps out and defends the wing (2). There is no bump down. On the pass from the

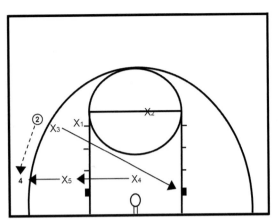

Diagram 7.6 Deep X Move

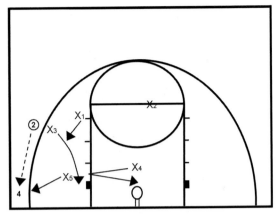

Diagram 7.7 Shallow X Move

wing (2) to the corner (4), X_3 drops back and covers the low post area. X_5 slides to the corner and defends the ball handler. X_4 holds at the low post until X_3 arrives and then moves to the weak side for rebounding position. X_1 can either block the lane or plug the middle using the box move.

High Post Coverage

It is important to keep the ball out of the high post area. When the ball is at the point and there is an offensive player in the high post, X_5 slides up and defends this player. It is also important that X_5 gets help from the defensive guard who is the back-defender. The defensive guard must have the arms extended in order to discourage the pass into the high post.

Elbows and Boxes Rule

The rule in the 2-3 zone defense is that the middle defender, X_5, covers the high post. Whenever the ball is at the high post, both boxes and elbows must be defended. This is called the "elbows and boxes rule." (See Diagram 7.8.)

When the ball is at the point and there is a high post, the defenders have the following responsibilities: #11 is the up-defender, #14 is the back-defender, #43 is in the "cheat position," #23 is responsible for the high post, and #24 is above the box and straddles the lane line.

2-3 Zone Slides

Using the whole method of teaching, the defenders learn their basic slides and individual responsibilities playing against five offensive players. Initially, the offensive players stay relatively stationary. As the defenders become skilled in the proper slides, the offense can begin attacking the zone. Eventually, additional offensive players are positioned on the floor. Diagrams 7.9 through 7.21 illustrate five defensive players defending eight offensive players.

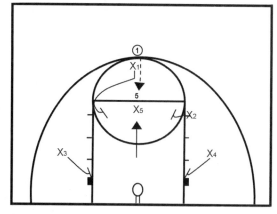

Diagram 7.8 Elbows and Boxes Rule

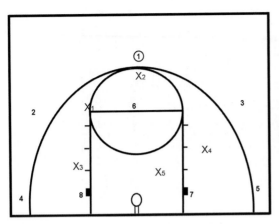

Diagram 7.9 Ball at the Point (X₂ Up-Defender)

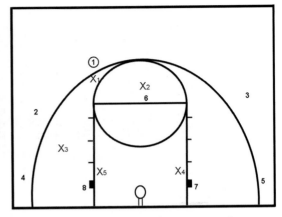

Diagram 7.10 Ball at the Point (X₁ Up-Defender)

Ball at the Point

Diagram 7.9 illustrates the location of the defense when the ball is at the point and X_2 is the up-defender.

- X_2 defends the ball handler.
- X_1 drops to the elbow area.
- X_4 cheats up and anticipates sliding out to defend a pass to the wing (3).
- X_3 and X_5 are positioned above the blocks and their responsibilities are similar to the back-line defenders in the 3-2 zone.

Diagram 7.10 shows the defense when X_1 is the up-defender and the ball is off the point.

- X_1 defends the ball handler.
- X_2 is the back-defender and discourages a pass to the high post.
- X_3 is in the cheat position.
- X_4 and X_5 are positioned above the blocks.

The defenders show the correct floor position after the ball has been passed from the point to the wing. (#14 was the up-defender.)

Pass from the Point to the Wing

Diagram 7.11 shows the slides of the defensive players when the ball is passed from the point to the wing and X_2 is the up-defender.

- X_1 slides out and crowds the ball handler.
- X_2 covers the elbow and keeps the ball out of the high post area.
- X_3 moves to a floor position halfway between the low post and the corner and anticipates a pass to 4.
- X_5 guards the low post area and is looking to defend flash cutters to the strong side box.
- X_4 slides down and protects against the lob pass or a crosscourt pass.

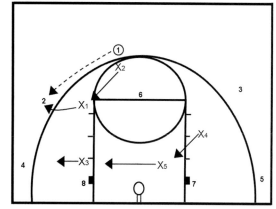

Diagram 7.11 Pass from the Point to the Wing

Coach Casey watches from behind the basket as the defenders show the correct floor position after the ball has been passed from the wing to the corner. #14 is "blocking the lane."

Pass from the Wing to the Corner

Diagram 7.12 illustrates the defensive slides when the ball is passed from the wing (2) to the corner (4).

- X_3 slides out and defends 4.
- X_1 can either block the lane and deny the pass back to the wing or plug the middle. Here, X_1 plugs the middle in order to keep the ball out of the medium post area.
- X_2 stays at the elbow until X_1 completes his or her slide and then moves to a position to stop the diagonal pass. X_5 defends the strong side box. X_4 is the weak side rebounder and guards against the lob pass or crosscourt pass.

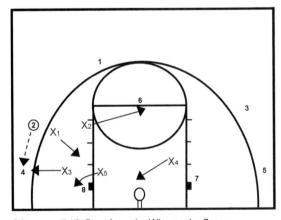

Diagram 7.12 Pass from the Wing to the Corner

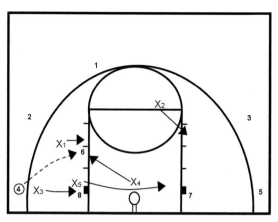

Diagram 7.13 Pass from the Corner to the Side Post (Option #1)

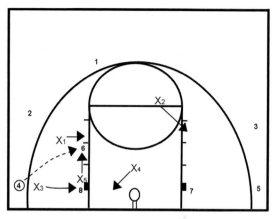

Diagram 7.14 Pass from the Corner to the Side Post (Option #2)

Pass from the Corner to the Side Post

Diagram 7.13 shows the defensive coverage when the ball is passed from the corner (4) to the side post (6).

- X_4 slides up to guard 6.
- X_3 slides back to the strong side box area.
- X_5 moves across the lane.
- X_2 is protecting against the diagonal pass.
- X_1 either protects the elbow and wing area or double-teams the side post.

There are situations that it may be best to have X_5 slide up and defend 6. X_4 would defend the post area. (See Diagram 7.14.)

Pass from the Point to the Corner

The defensive slides when X_2 is the up-defender and the ball is passed from the point (1) to the corner (5) are shown in Diagram 7.15.

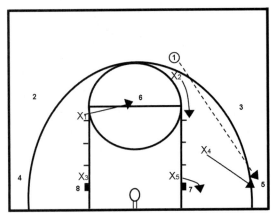

Diagram 7.15 Pass from the Point to the Corner

- X_4 slides from the cheat position to the corner and defends 5.
- X_2 covers the elbow area (or can block the lane defending on the defensive coverage).
- X_1 straddles the free throw line (or covers the elbow if X_2 blocks the lane).
- X_5 slides to the strong side box area.
- X_3 is the weak side rebounder.

Pass from the Point to the Wing (Bump Move)

Diagram 7.16 illustrates the slides when the ball is passed from the point (1) to the wing (3).

- X_4, who was in the cheat position, slides out to "bother" 3 and stop a three-point shot.
- X_2 drops to the elbow momentarily and then quickly slides out to cover 3. This initiates the bump down between X_2 and X_4. X_4 drops back, faces the ball, and is ready to cover a pass to the corner.
- X_3 moves into the lane in front of the basket.
- X_5 defends the strong side box area.
- X_1 straddles the free throw line.

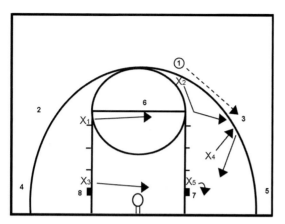

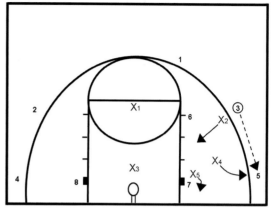

Diagram 7.16 Pass from the Point to the Wing (Bump Move)

Diagram 7.17 Pass from the Wing to the Corner

Pass from the Wing to the Corner

The defensive coverage when the ball is passed from the wing (3) to the corner (5) is shown in Diagram 7.17.

- X_4 guards the ball in the corner.
- X_5 defends the strong side box area.
- X_3 is the weak side rebounder.
- X_2 prevents a pass into the side post.
- X_1 straddles the free throw line and anticipates the diagonal pass.

Pass from the Wing to the Elbow

Diagram 7.18 illustrates the defensive slides when the ball is quickly passed from the point (1) to the wing (3) and then to the elbow (6).

- X_4 was sliding from the cheat position to the wing when the pass was made. X_4 must quickly retreat and cover the strong side box.
- X_5 comes up to guard the ball at the elbow.
- X_3 defends the weak side box.
- X_2 slides to the elbow area and can dig at the ball.
- X_1 covers the weak side elbow.

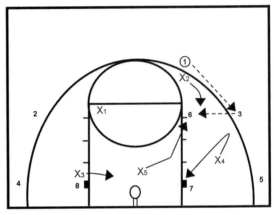

Diagram 7.18 Pass from the Wing to the Elbow

Another way to defend the quick pass from the wing to the elbow is illustrated in Diagram 7.19. Instead of X_5 coming up and guarding the ball at the elbow, X_3 breaks up and defends 6. X_5 then moves to cover the weak side box area.

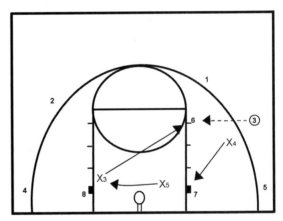

Diagram 7.19 Pass from the Wing to the Elbow (Alternative)

Pass from the Point to the High Post

The defensive slides when the ball is passed from the point (1) to the high post (6) are shown in Diagram 7.20. Whenever the ball is in the high post, the elbows and boxes rule is in effect.

- The middle defender, X_5, quickly moves up to defend the high post (6).
- X_4 and X_3 defend against any passes to the box areas.
- X_1 and X_2 defend the elbow areas.

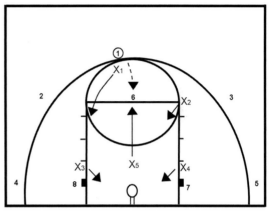

Diagram 7.20 Pass from the Point to the High Post

Pass from the High Post to the Corner

Diagram 7.21 illustrates the defensive coverage when the ball is passed from the high post (6) to the corner (5).

- X_4 slides out and covers the ball handler.
- X_2 plugs the middle.
- The back-line defender, X_3, slides across the lane and defends the strong side box area.
- X_5 drops back and is the weak side rebounder.
- X_1 straddles the free throw line while facing the ball.

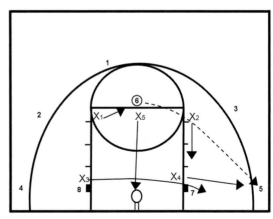

Diagram 7.21 Pass from the High Post to the Corner

Rebound Positions

Rebounding responsibilities in a 2-3 zone are very similar to the 3-2 zone. When a shot is taken, the principle of "elbows, boxes, and middle of the lane" prevails. These five spots must be filled on every shot attempt. It is also essential that the front-line defenders block out any offensive players charging down the lane for the offensive rebound.

Shot from the Point

Diagram 7.22 illustrates the rebounding positions when the ball is shot from the point.

- X_1 blocks out the shooter and then moves to the elbow area.
- X_2 rebounds the elbow area on the other side of the court.
- X_3 and X_4 are responsible for rebounding their respective box areas.
- X_5 is the middle-of-the-lane rebounder.

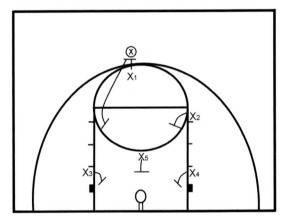

Diagram 7.22 Shot from the Point

Shot from the Wing

Diagram 7.23 shows the rebounding positions when the ball is shot from the wing.

- X_2 blocks out the shooter and then moves to the elbow.
- X_1 rebounds the weak side elbow area.
- X_4 covers the strong side box area.
- X_3 rebounds the weak side box area.
- X_5 rebounds the middle area of the lane.

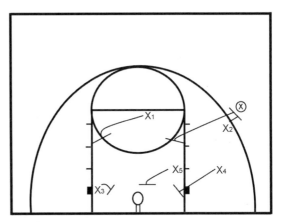

Diagram 7.23 Shot from the Wing

Shot from the Corner

Diagram 7.24 shows the rebounding positions when the ball is shot from the corner.

- X_4 blocks out the shooter and proceeds to the box area.
- X_5 covers the strong side box first and then moves to the middle of the lane.
- X_3 rebounds the weak side box.
- X_1 moves to the weak side elbow.
- X_2 covers the strong side elbow.

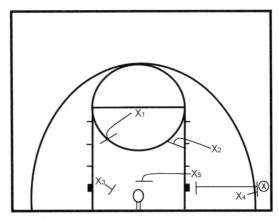

Diagram 7.24 Shot from the Corner

8
Advanced Training

The successful basketball coach continually searches for innovative strategies to stop today's talented players and high-powered offenses. Winning teams control the tempo of the game, and one of the best ways to do this is with a zone defense. No opponent should feel completely comfortable and confident when attacking a zone defense. Every coach must have tactics within his or her defensive arsenal to stop the momentum of an opponent.

The material in Chapter 8 provides advanced techniques that will create confusion among opposing players and stifle an offensive attack. These tactics, if used properly, will neutralize talent and increase the likelihood of defeating a superior opponent.

Lead-Up Drills

The best way to prepare players for advanced defensive training is to put them in an outnumbering situation because it requires players to communicate and identify the most dangerous offensive players. After mastering the individual defensive fundamentals, players should be introduced to the 2 vs. 1, 3 vs. 2, and 5 vs. 4 drills.

2 vs. 1 Drill

As shown in Diagram 8.1, the offensive players attempt to stay wide and score a layup shot as quickly as possible. The defender, X_1, must prevent the easy basket and slow down the offensive attack until defensive help arrives. To accomplish this, X_1 employs a delaying action known as the "fake and fade." X_1 fakes toward the offensive ball handler and then drops back to protect the basket area. X_1's primary job is to stop an uncontested drive to the basket and delay the offense until his or her teammates can get back.

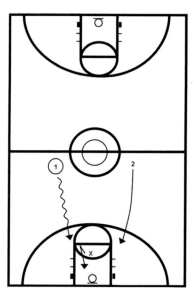

Diagram 8.1 2 vs. 1 Drill

2 vs. 1 Plus 1 Drill

After learning the fake-and-fade maneuver, add another defensive player to this drill to emphasize the importance of defensive transition. In Diagram 8.2, X_2 begins on the opposite baseline. When the offensive players begin their attack on X_1, X_2 sprints back as quickly as possible to help X_1.

3 vs. 2 Drill

The next progression is three offensive players attacking two defenders. Many coaches think of the 3 vs. 2 only in reference to the fast break, but it occurs in many other situations. John Egli, one of the leading proponents of the zone defense in the 1950s and 1960s, considered this drill to be the backbone of the sliding zone defense.

As shown in Diagram 8.3, three offensive players attempt to score on two defenders. X_1 and X_2 form a tandem. X_1 attempts to stop the ball handler (1) by using the fake-and-fade maneuver. X_2 anticipates guarding the player who receives the pass from 1.

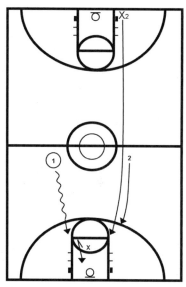

Diagram 8.2 2 vs. 1 Plus 1 Drill

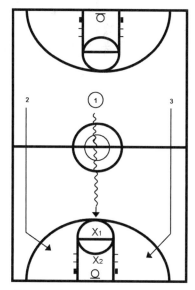

Diagram 8.3 3 vs. 2 Drill

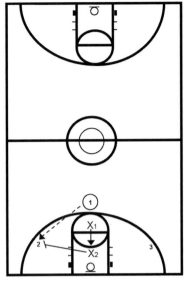

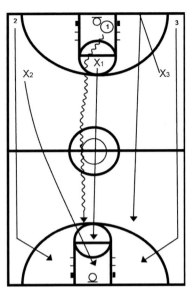

Diagram 8.4 3 vs. 2 Drill (Pass to the Wing)

Diagram 8.5 3 vs. 2 Plus 1 Drill

In Diagram 8.4, 1 passes to 2. X_2 slides out to defend the ball handler. X_1 quickly drops back into the lane and protects the basket area. X_1's first step must be straight back. Many defenders have the tendency to move toward the first pass, and this erroneous movement creates a split-second opening for the offensive team to pass the ball inside for an easy score. On each succeeding pass, one defensive player will take the ball handler while the other defender will take a position near the basket and prevent any layup shots.

3 vs. 2 Plus 1 Drill

The 3 vs. 2 plus 1 drill incorporates an outnumbering situation and defensive transition. Three offensive players are positioned on the baseline and three defenders are spread out on the free throw line extended. The drill begins when a coach calls out the name of one of the defenders. In Diagram 8.5, this player is X_3. X_3 touches the baseline and then sprints back on defense. The two other defensive players (X_1 and X_2) sprint back, set a defensive tandem, and slow down the offensive attack until their teammate (X_3) can get back. The offensive players are advancing the ball as quickly as possible and attempting to score.

5 vs. 4 Drill

The four-player zone is not only an excellent defensive tactic but also an outstanding defensive drill. In the 5 vs. 4 drill, four defenders are required to stop five offensive players. Diagram 8.6 shows the floor location of the four defenders. The four-player zone combines slides from the 3-2 zone and the 2-3 zone. Defenders X_1 and X_2 adhere to the front-line rules for the 2-3 zone defense that were described in Chapter 7. Defenders X_3

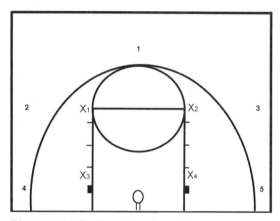

Diagram 8.6 The Four-Player Zone Defense

and X_4 follow the back-line rules for the 3-2 zone defense that were explained in Chapter 6.

The offensive players are initially positioned at the point, wings, side post, and short corner and remain relatively stationary. Diagram 8.7 shows the defensive coverage when the ball is at the point. X_1 and X_2 must see the floor, identify the most dangerous offensive players, and communicate which one will take the ball handler. In this case, it is best that X_2 becomes the up-defender because X_1 should remain at the elbow and prevent the pass being thrown directly to the side post (4).

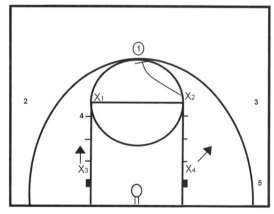

Diagram 8.7 Ball at the Point

Diagram 8.8 shows the ball being passed from the point (1) to the wing (2).

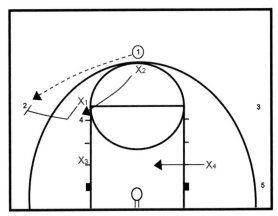

Diagram 8.8 Pass from the Point to the Wing

- X$_2$ quickly slides over and defends the elbow area. X$_2$ must adjust his or her floor position depending on the location of the side post (4).
- X$_1$ protects the elbow until X$_2$ arrives and then slides out and guards the wing (2).
- X$_3$ and X$_4$ slide in the direction of the next most dangerous player in their area.

Trapping

It is essential for any team that hopes to surprise an opponent to be able to trap out of any of their defenses. The fundamentals for trapping are the same for both man-to-man and zone defenses. Although only two defenders execute the trap, the entire defensive team must react if trapping is going to be successful. The three defenders that are not trapping create a triangle consisting of two floaters and one defender protecting the basket. As long as the basket is protected, any defense can afford the risk involved.

Trapping Rules

There are five basic trap situations in any kind of defense: the guard-to-guard, the guard-to-forward, the forward-to-guard, the forward-to-post, and the guard-to-post. The trap is built on the elements of quickness and surprise, and all defenders should adhere to the following rules.

- **The Three-Step Rule.** The defender who goes to trap must be able to reach the ball handler in three quick steps or less.
- **No-Splitting-the-Trap Rule.** The defenders must assume a wide base and place one of their feet as close as possible to their trapping teammate.
- **The No-Fouling Rule.** The trappers should not slap at the ball or foul the ball handler.
- **The Active-Hands Rule.** The defenders must keep their hands active and play for deflections.

The trappers should have active hands and not allow the ball handler to split the double team.

When to Trap

Defenders must become adept at recognizing when to trap. Some of the best times to trap include the following situations: a pick-and-roll; a dribble weave; a guard-outside situation (the guard passes to the wing and follows his or her pass for a return hand-off); a pass to a post player; and a ball handler dribbling toward the corner. When a team knows when and how to trap, there are many trapping tactics that can be used with any type of defense.

Guidelines for Trapping

Hubie Brown, two-time NBA Coach of the Year and Hall of Fame coach, believes there must be guidelines for trapping, but coaches should be flexible and allow players to be creative. Brown has identified the most important principles for trapping in today's games.

- The best places to trap are near the sidelines, baseline, corners, and half-court line.
- Belly up and seal on double-teams.
- Never let the ball handler split the trap.
- Once committed to trapping, don't stop or hesitate and get caught in no-man's land.
- Teach your players off the ball to read the eyes and position of the player being trapped.
- When trapping, leave the defender farthest from the ball free.
- Don't let weak side offensive players flash-cut to the ball as outlets.
- Practice weak side rotation.
- Stay in the double team until the pass is released and in the air.
- Don't allow a penetrating pass out of the trap.
- If you force the pass backward, zone up and continue to trap.
- Stay attached to shooters—lock in and don't permit them to get free.

Joe Chapman (#32) seals the double team with Marcus Jackson (#35) and is in the belly-up position.

3-2 Zone Trap

The 3-2 zone trap can be either an aggressive or passive defense. Both are needed in your defensive arsenal because every opponent poses different challenges. There is not one defense that will work against every team on your schedule.

Hard 3-2 Trap Defense

During the 1950s, John Egli from Penn State developed a half-court 3-2 zone press based on his sliding zone principles. Penn State's half-court zone press looked very much like a nonpressing defense but quickly changed to an active and aggressive defensive attack once the ball approached the midcourt line. Egli's half-court trap often caught opponents off-guard and created several turnovers before the offense made the necessary adjustments. He believed it was an excellent way to control the pace of a game.

Coauthor Casey used Egli's 3-2 zone principles as his foundation and then expanded the concepts to create various stunts. When using the 3-2 zone trap, it is important to keep the ball out of the middle of the floor and the post area. Once the ball gets into the high post, it can easily be passed to either side of the floor, and it makes the defensive coverage twice as difficult. Defenders must become skilled at forcing the ball to the sidelines and the corners because it creates excellent trapping opportunities. In addition, the location of these traps limits the areas of attack for the offensive team and allows the three defenders who are not trapping to position themselves where they have a better chance of intercepting a pass.

Diagram 8.9 shows the initial alignment of the defenders and the midcourt trap.

- X_1, X_2, and X_3 quickly extend the defense as the ball advances toward midcourt.
- X_1 and X_2 become the trappers once the dribbler establishes a strong side of the floor and crosses the midcourt line.
- X_3, who had moved out toward the midcourt line on the initial movement of the defense, now retreats to the middle of the floor and becomes an interceptor.
- X_4 moves out to the wing area and denies any direct passes into this area.
- X_5 moves up and stops a pass into the post.

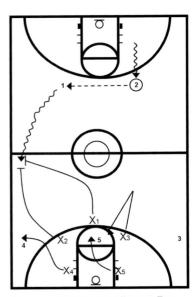

Diagram 8.9 The 3-2 Midcourt Trap

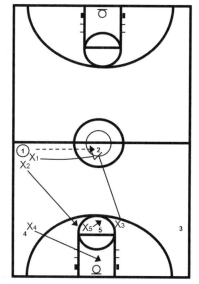

Diagram 8.10 Pass from 1 to 2

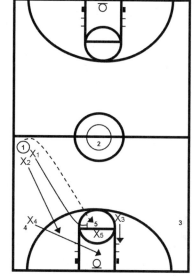

Diagram 8.11 Pass from 1 to 5

Diagram 8.10 illustrates the defensive slides when the ball is passed from 1 to 2.

- X_1 follows the pass and executes a trap with X_3.
- X_5 fronts any offensive player in the high post.
- X_4 slides down and protects the basket area.
- X_2 drops back toward the elbow.

Diagram 8.11 shows the defensive coverage when the ball is passed from 1 to 5.

- X_5 defends 5 using man-to-man fundamentals.
- X_1 double-teams the high post with X_5.
- X_3 drops and is responsible for any pass to his or her side of the court. The reference point for the depth of the drop is to be on an imaginary line drawn from the ball handler and the corner.
- X_4 slides back and protects the basket area.
- X_2 drops and is responsible for any pass to his or her side of the court.

Diagram 8.12 shows the defensive slides when the ball is passed from 1 to 4.

- X_4 defends 4 using man-to-man fundamentals.
- X_2 double-teams the ball handler with X_4.
- X_5 guards any player in the side post area.
- X_1 drops back to the middle of the floor.
- X_3 defends the basket area.

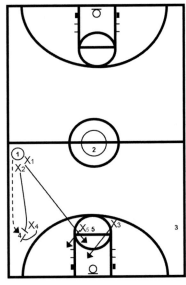

Diagram 8.12 Pass from 1 to 4

Soft 3-2 Zone Trap

The 3-2 zone trap can provide many benefits even if it is not creating turnovers. If the defense is taking opponents out of their desired tempo, exposing weak ball handlers, or bringing "life" to your players, then it is serving a worthwhile purpose. Be careful not to assess your zone trap only on steals.

The soft 3-2 trap defense is a tactic that is designed to take opponents out of their offensive rhythm. It also sends a message to your opponent that you can come after them when you want to. The trap may take place at the wing, corner, or post. It is usually a "one and done" trap.

2-3 Zone Trap

The initial alignment of the 2-3 zone trap is identical to the regular 2-3 zone defense. The element of surprise does not begin until the ball is passed from the point to the wing. At this point, the back-line defender traps the ball rather than executing the bump down move. Diagrams 8.13 through 8.24 illustrate the defensive slides and trapping opportunities as the ball is passed from one area to the next.

Wing Trap (After the Pass from the Point)

Diagram 8.13 shows the wing trap after the ball is passed from the point.

- X$_1$ protects the high post first and then quickly traps the wing (3).
- X$_3$ moves out and traps the wing (3).
- X$_2$ moves across the free throw line and defends the elbow.
- X$_5$ is in the cheat position.
- X$_4$ is positioned in front of the basket and protects against the lob pass.

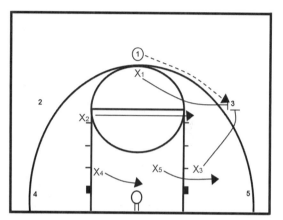

Diagram 8.13 Pass from the Point to the Wing Trap

Corner Trap (After the Pass from the Wing)

Diagram 8.14 illustrates the corner trap after the pass from the wing.

- X$_3$ follows the pass to the corner and traps with X$_5$.
- X$_1$ either blocks the lane (shown in Diagram 8.10 on page 143) or plugs the middle.
- X$_2$ protects the high post area and is defending against the diagonal pass.
- X$_5$ slides out and traps the ball handler (5).
- X$_4$ slides in front of the box.

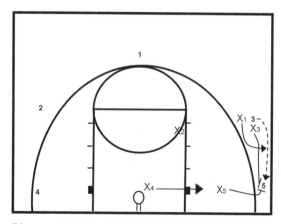

Diagram 8.14 Pass from the Wing to the Corner Trap

Pass from the Corner Trap to the Point

Diagram 8.15 shows the floor position of the defenders when the ball is passed from the corner to the point.

- X_2 slides out and is positioned on the outside shoulder of the ball handler (1).
- X_1 becomes the wing defender.
- X_4 moves to the cheat position.
- X_5 hustles across the lane to the box area.
- X_3 slides to the weak side block area.

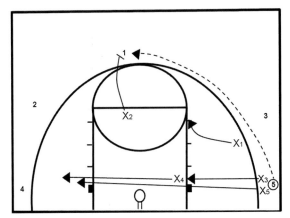

Diagram 8.15 Pass from the Corner Trap to the Point

Wing Trap (After the Pass from the Point)

Diagram 8.16 shows the wing trap after the ball has been passed from the corner to the point, and then to the wing.

- X_2 slides to the high post and then moves out and traps the wing (2) with X_4.
- X_4 moves out and traps the wing (2).
- X_1 moves across the free throw line and defends the elbow.
- X_5 is in the cheat position.
- X_3 is positioned in front of the basket and protects against the lob pass.

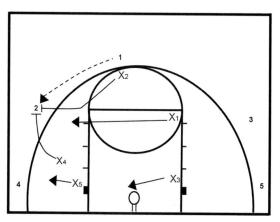

Diagram 8.16 Pass from the Point to the Wing Trap

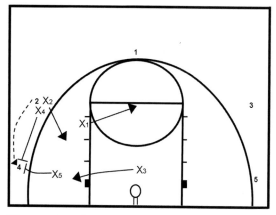

Diagram 8.17 Pass from Wing to the Corner Trap

Corner Trap (After the Pass from the Wing)

Diagram 8.17 shows the corner trap after the ball is passed from the wing.

- X_4 follows the pass to the corner and traps with X_5.
- X_2 either plugs the middle (shown in Diagram 8.17) or blocks the lane.
- X_1 protects the high post area and is defending against the diagonal pass.
- X_5 slides out and traps the ball handler (4).
- X_3 slides in front of the box.

Pass from the Corner Trap to the Point (Alternate Slide)

Diagram 8.18 offers an alternate way to cover the pass from the corner trap to the point as compared to Diagram 8.15.

- X_2 moves toward the wing in an attempt to delay a quick ball reversal.
- X_1 becomes the point defender and attacks the ball handler's outside shoulder.

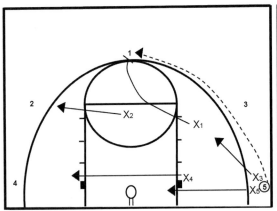
Diagram 8.18 Pass from the Corner Trap to the Point (Alternative Slide)

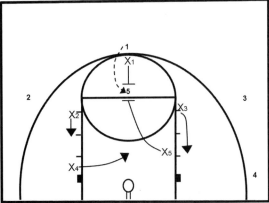
Diagram 8.19 Pass from the Point to the High Post

- X_3 moves to the cheat position on the wing.
- X_4 slides across and straddles the lane.
- X_5 straddles the lane as the back-defender of the zone.

High Post Trap (After the Pass from the Point)

Diagram 8.19 illustrates the high post trap after the ball is passed from the point.

- X_1 turns and traps the high post (5) with X_5.
- X_2 drops slightly below the level of the ball.
- X_3 is split between the wing (3) and the corner (4).
- X_5 slides up and traps the high post (5) with X_1.
- X_4 protects the lane area.

Wing Trap (After the Pass from the High Post)

Diagram 8.20 shows the wing trap after the ball is passed from the high post.

- X_3 slides up, keeps 3 from dribbling toward the corner, and traps with X_1.
- X_1 follows the pass and traps with X_3.
- X_4 fronts the box area.
- X_5 drops to the middle of the lane and protects against the lob.
- X_2 hustles across the lane and defends the elbow area.

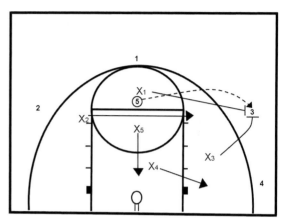

Diagram 8.20 Pass from the High Post to the Wing Trap

Corner Trap (After the Pass from the Wing)

Diagram 8.21 shows the corner trap after the ball is passed from the wing (3) to the corner (4).

- X_4 slides out, guards the ball handler, and sets a trap with X_3.
- X_3 follows the pass and traps with X_4.
- X_5 moves in front of box.
- X_1 either blocks the lane or plugs the middle. Here X_1 is plugging the middle.
- X_2 covers the high post and defends against the diagonal pass.

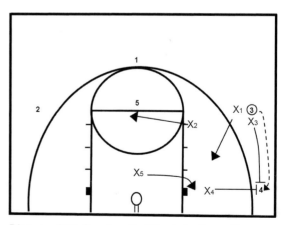

Diagram 8.21 Pass from the Wing to the Corner Trap

Corner Trap (After a Pass from the High Post Trap)

Some coaches believe that it is too difficult to go from the high post trap to a corner trap, while others believe that it can be very advantageous. Diagram 8.22 illustrates one method of defending the box area when the ball is passed from a high post trap to the corner.

- X_2 traps topside with X_4.
- X_4 slides out to the corner and traps the ball handler with X_2.
- X_1 defends the elbow area.
- X_5 defends the box area.
- X_3 moves to the middle of the lane in front of the basket.

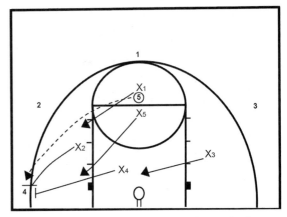

Diagram 8.22 Pass from the High Post Trap to the Corner (Option #1)

A second method of trapping the ball in the corner is shown in Diagram 8.23. The responsibilities of X_1, X_2, and X_4 remain the same while X_3 and X_5 adhere to the following guidelines:

- X_3 defends the box area.
- X_5 slides down to the middle of the lane in front of the basket.

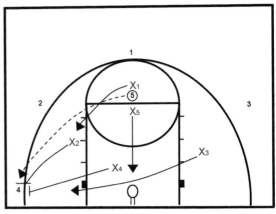

Diagram 8.23 Pass from the High Post Trap to the Corner (Option #2)

Pass from the Corner Trap to the Point

Diagram 8.24 shows the pass to the point from the corner trap.

- X_1 slides up and defends the ball handler.
- X_2 covers the elbow area.
- X_4 straddles the free throw lane line.
- X_3 loops under X_5 and assumes the cheat position.
- X_5 straddles the free throw lane line.

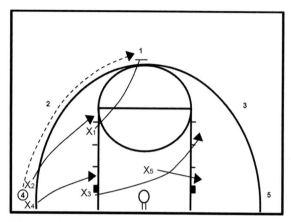

Diagram 8.24 Pass from the Corner Trap to the Point

Note: Defenders X_3 and X_5 can switch slide assignments.

Jack Greynolds's 1-1-2-1 Half-Court Trap

During the 1960s, Jack Greynolds's Revere High School teams dominated the Suburban League in Akron, Ohio. Greynolds was a master at creating defenses that maximized the talents of his players. His teams at Revere stifled superior opponents with an innovative 1-1-2-1 half-court press and aggressive 2-3 zone defense. Greynolds's creativity was ignited from Neal Baisi's pressing defenses and John McLendon's "fast breaking defense." Diagram 8.25 illustrates the initial alignment of the 1-1-2-1 half-court trap.

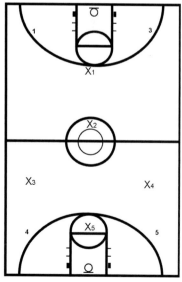

Diagram 8.25 Initial Alignment of the 1-1-2-1 Half-Court Trap

Diagram 8.26 shows the defensive coverage as the ball handler dribbles toward the midcourt line.

- X₁'s primary responsibilities are to keep the ball out of the middle of the floor and lead the ball handler (1) into a trap as soon as the ball is dribbled across the midcourt line.
- X₂ is the interceptor and defends against any flash cut to the middle of the court.
- X₃ traps the ball handler.
- X₅ defends against the sideline pass from 1 to 4.
- X₄ protects the basket area.

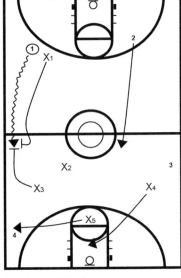

Diagram 8.26 Trap

Many offenses will use a two-guard front and try to reverse the ball quickly and then attack the zone press. To counter this tactic, X₁ and X₂ exchange responsibilities. Diagram 8.27 illustrates the defensive coverage when the ball is reversed.

- X₂ moves up and becomes the point defender.
- X₁ slides into the interceptor position.
- X₄ moves up and traps the ball handler with X₂.
- X₅ defends against the sideline pass.
- X₃ protects the basket area.

3-2 Defensive Stunts

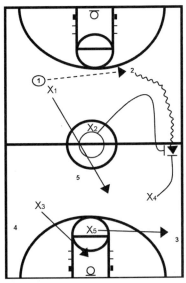

Diagram 8.27 Ball Reversal

The 3-2 zone defense is one of the most flexible and versatile defenses being used today. With minor adjustments, the 3-2 zone can successfully counter most of today's zone offensive attacks. The defensive stunts introduced in this chapter will not work against all teams. Each one is designed as a countermove to an offensive strength and provides a short-term option to change the momentum of a game.

Stunts with the Point Defender

The point defender, X_1, is in one of the most advantageous floor positions from which to stunt. By altering X_1's defensive assignments, the 3-2 zone can take on many different looks.

Point Defender Drop. The "point defender drop" was popular in the 1980s and has recently resurfaced. It can be used with the 3-2, 1-2-2, or a flat 3-2 zone defense. The major advantage of the point defender drop is that it allows for better rebounding coverage because it always keeps one of your best rebounders on the weak side. When using this stunt, it is important to have a taller defender at the point because this player will have to be able to rebound and defend a low post. As the ball is passed from the point to the wing and then to the corner, the point defender (X_1) must always be positioned on an imaginary line drawn from the ball to the basket. Diagram 8.28 shows the point defender drop as the ball is passed from the point to the wing, and then to the corner.

When the ball is in the corner, the strong side defensive wing (X_3) must block the lane in order to prevent quick ball reversal. This allows X_1 sufficient time to get from the box to the point and stop a three-point shooter when the ball is reversed. Another key is

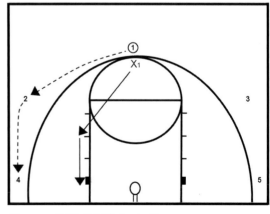

Diagram 8.28 Point Defender Drop

for the strong side back-line defender to pressure the ball handler in the corner and stop the skip pass from the corner to the point.

Another option that many coaches prefer is for the point defender (X_1) to become a back-line defender once the ball has initially left the point. This variation changes the alignment of the defense from a 3-2 to a 2-3 with the point defender (X_1) becoming the middle defender of the 2-3 zone defense. This coverage makes it much easier to defend against ball reversal.

Wings Out Point Drops. Diagram 8.29 illustrates the "wings out point drops" defensive stunt. This maneuver can be very effective against an offensive team that uses a two-guard front where both guards are excellent perimeter shooters. It requires a taller point defender who can also play good post defense. As the offensive team advances the ball, the point defender (X_1) slides down the lane

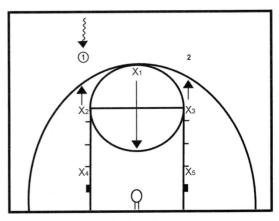

Diagram 8.29 Wing Out Point Drops

while the defensive wings, X_2 and X_3, move up toward the top of the circle. The alignment of the 3-2 zone now changes to a 2-1-2 zone. The slides also change from a 3-2 zone to a 2-3 zone coverage.

Point Chaser. The "point chaser" stunt is shown in Diagram 8.30. It is very effective against a team that sends an excellent shooting guard through the zone to the corner. Whenever 2 cuts through the zone, X_1 begins his or her

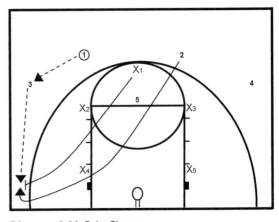

Diagram 8.30 Point Chaser

man-to-man coverage. The rest of the players are in a four-person zone defense. The defensive wings follow the front-line rules for the 2-3 zone defense, and the X_4 and X_5 defenders adhere to the backline rules for the 3-2 zone defense.

Flat 3-2 Zone Defense

The Detroit Pistons effectively used a "flat 3-2 zone defense" against the Miami Heat in the 2006 NBA Eastern Conference Finals. Detroit initially went to a traditional 3-2 zone defense and the Heat countered by going to a "point screen" offense. The Pistons then dropped the point defender to the free throw line so that the 3-2 zone was completely flat. (See Diagram 8.31.) This

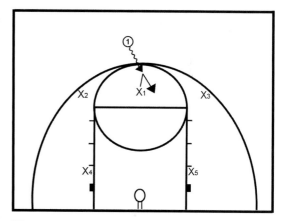

Diagram 8.31 Flat 3-2 Zone Defense

maneuver utilized many of the defensive concepts from Doc Meanwell's two-line defense that was created in the 1910s and was discussed in Chapter 2.

The Pistons' flat 3-2 zone took Miami out of their point screen offense, limited the number of passes that could be thrown into Shaquille O'Neal, and stopped Dwyane Wade's penetration. Whenever an offensive ball handler was at the top of the circle, X_1 utilized the fake-and-fade maneuver to prevent any wide-open shots. The flat 3-2 zone helped the Pistons claw back from a double-digit deficit and limited Wade to one shot during an entire quarter.

Defending Against the 1-4 Zone Offense

Many opposing coaches design their zone offenses so that they distort the zone defense. One of the best ways to do this is with a 1-4 zone offense. Teams that use a 1-4 offense generally place their best shooters on the wings, their post players at the elbows, and their best ball handler and passer at the point. In the following diagrams, the best way to match up against the 1-4 zone offense will be illustrated and explained.

Diagram 8.32 shows the traditional 3-2 zone defense against a 1-4 alignment. It is easily seen that there is a 4-on-2 advantage for the offense across the free throw line extended.

Diagram 8.33 illustrates the defensive adjustment that must be made in order to combat the advantage of the 1-4 offense.

- X_1 must influence the ball handler to one side of the floor. This is critical to the success of the defense. It is also important to know which side of the floor the ball handler should be influenced. This will be determined from your scouting reports.
- X_3 slides out and covers the strong side wing (2).

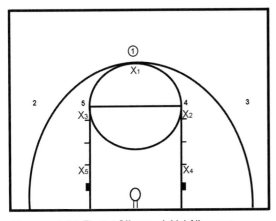

Diagram 8.32 The 1-4 Offense—Initial Alignment

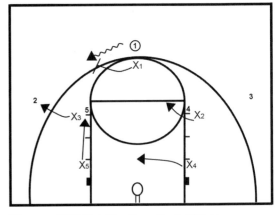

Diagram 8.33 Matching Up vs. the 1-4 Offense

- X_5 moves up and defends the strong side high post player (5).
- X_2 slides across the lane and fronts the weak side high post player (4).
- X_4 slides up toward the middle of the lane and protects the basket area. X_4 must also defend against any lob pass.

Diagram 8.34 illustrates the defensive floor positions after the ball has been passed from the point (1) to the wing (2). The defense is designed to pressure the ball handler and keep the ball on one side of the floor. All passing lanes on the ball side of the floor are denied and the only open offensive player is the weak side wing.

Diagram 8.35 shows the defenders after the ball is thrown crosscourt from 2 to 3.

- X_2 slides out and defends 3. X_2 must anticipate the crosscourt pass and not get caught by a screen set by 4.
- X_4 quickly slides up and defends the strong side high post.
- X_5 moves down to protect the basket area and stop any lob pass.
- X_1 denies the pass to the point guard (1).
- X_3 slides across the lane and fronts 5.

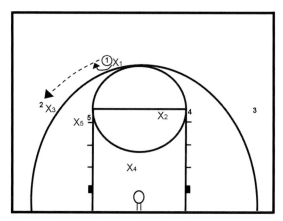

Diagram 8.34 Pass from the Point to the Wing

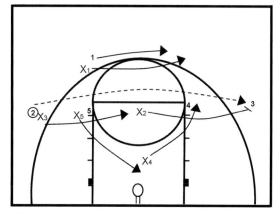

Diagram 8.35 Crosscourt Pass

Defending Against the Pick-and-Roll

The biggest change in zone offenses over the past decade is the increased use of screening on the ball. Prior to this time, most zone offensives were based on the principles of proper spacing and cutting, and very seldom was there a screen set for the ball handler. Today, the best offensive teams are also the best pick-and-roll teams. To beat these teams, you must be able to defend against the pick-and-roll. This often presents a major challenge because the pick-and-roll is the most difficult play to stop in basketball. The concept of the pick-and-roll is illustrated in Diagram 8.36.

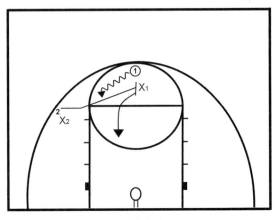

Diagram 8.36 Pick-and-Roll Action

Pat Summitt, the NCAA all-time career victory leader, emphasizes the defensive coverage of the pick-and-roll during the first month of every season. Her defensive teaching includes the following points:

- The defender on the ball handler must force the dribbler to use the screen. Do not give the ball handler an option.
- The screener's defender must step out aggressively and "show his or her numbers" to the dribbler using the screen. This tactic is called a "heavy hedge" and is similar to a fake trap. For a split second, many people will think you are trapping the ball.

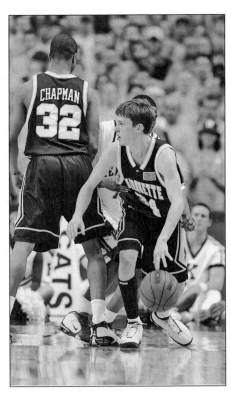

The pick-and-roll is the hardest play to defend in basketball.

- Once the dribbler's defender gets back in front of the ball, the screener's defender recovers.
- If the screener slips the pick, the defender guarding the screener must go also. The teaching point is for the defender to "keep a hand on the back" of the screener. This enables the defender to know exactly where the screener is at all times.

Five Ways to Defend the Pick-and-Roll

There are five ways that you can defend the pick-and-roll. It is essential that your players become proficient in all of them, because there is a time and place for each technique.

1. Switch. The most popular technique used by zone defenders to guard the screen on the ball is the switch. This requires excellent communication and anticipation. As shown in Diagram 8.37, X_2, the defender guarding the screener, "jumps out" into the path of the dribbler and defends against the outside shot and dribble penetration. The other defensive player quickly picks up the screener who will either be rolling to the basket or popping out to the perimeter.

Diagram 8.37 Switch

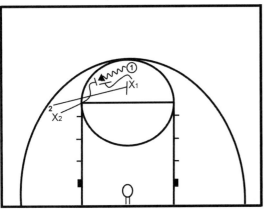

Diagram 8.38 Trap   **Diagram 8.39** Bump and Go Under

2. Trap. When you are trying to defend a great player like John Stockton, the best way to get the ball out of the superstar's hands is to trap. In Diagram 8.38, X_2 and X_1 double-team the ball handler. When using this technique, the guiding principle is that you trap with two players and zone with the other three. Your goal is to make the offense play on just one-half of the court. The only pass that should be allowed out of the trap is a lob pass.

3. Bump and Go Under. When defending against weak perimeter shooters, the best technique to use is the "bump and go under." As shown in Diagram 8.39, X_2 physically bumps 2 and forces the screen to be set farther from the basket. X_2 must also be ready to contest a shot. X_1 goes under the screen, then recovers to the ball handler.

4. Show and Go Over-Under. This technique is used to defend excellent perimeter shooters. As shown in Diagram 8.40, X_2, the defensive player guarding the screener, must step out, show his or her numbers, and make the dribbler go away from the basket. This defender contests any shot but does not stay with the dribbler for more than two dribbles. X_1, the defender on the dribbler, goes over the top of the screen but under his or her defensive teammate.

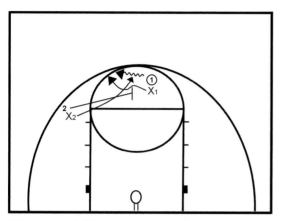

Diagram 8.40 Show and Go Over-Under

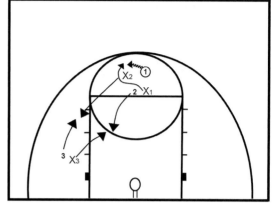

Diagram 8.41 X Move

5. **X.** The "X" is a continuation of the show and go over-under technique. If the screener quickly rolls to the basket, his or her defender, who had stepped out to slow down the dribbler, cannot recover in time to stop the pick-and-roll. The best way to defend this play is to use the "X" technique. (See Diagram 8.41.) The back-line defender (X_3) yells, "X!," and picks up the player rolling to the basket. The defender who had stepped out (X_2) guards the back-line defender's player or the most dangerous opponent.

3 vs. 3 Pick-and-Roll Drill

One the best ways to become proficient at stopping the pick-and-roll is to incorporate the 3 vs. 3 drill into your practice routine. This drill is an excellent way to teach the different ways to defend the pick-and-roll. The 3 vs. 3 pick-and-roll drill should be initiated run from the wing, elbow, corner, and top of the circle.

Hubie Brown's Defense Against the Pick-and-Roll

Hubie Brown's 2-3 zone defense against the San Antonio Spurs' pick-and-roll stymied the play of superstars Tony Parker and Tim Duncan. One of San Antonio's sets had Duncan break out to the wing and set a pick on Parker's defender. Parker would use the screen to create a scoring opportunity for himself or one of his teammates. The innovative Brown countered this tactic by putting his team in a 2-3 zone and having the middle defender, X_5, come out and shadow Parker as he used the screen set by Duncan. (See Diagram 8.42.) X_5's job was to force Parker to dribble away from the basket. This allowed X_2, who had fought over the top of the pick, to catch up and defend Parker. X_5 would then survey the situation and locate the most dangerous player as he slid back into the lane.

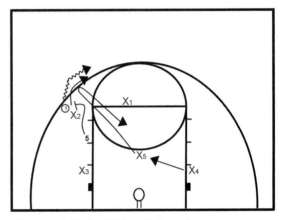

Diagram 8.42 The 2-3 Zone Defense Stunt

Brown's ingenious method of defending the pick-and-roll has sparked the imaginations of creative coaches. Utilizing one of the back-line defenders in the zone to break up and disrupt the timing of the pick-and-roll at the wing or point must be explored. It provides a new way to stop the most dangerous play in the game.

Hybrid Defenses

A hybrid defense combines elements of several different types of defenses and presents unique challenges for offenses. There is a definite time and place for hybrid defenses in the game of basketball. Do not hesitate using them for several possessions as a tempo changer or as an element of surprise. Too many coaches are reluctant to use them because they feel that they have not worked on them enough in practice. That may be true, but even more important is the question, "Is your opponent prepared to attack this defense?" The majority of the time an offensive team has very little or no experience attacking a hybrid defense.

Two of the most popular hybrid defenses are the box-and-one and the triangle-and-two. In 2007, the Memphis Grizzlies used the box-and-one on Kobe Bryant after he had four consecutive games of 50-plus points and held him to 23 points and won the game by two points. Bryant missed 19 of his 26 shot attempts. After the game Bryant said, "They played a box-and-one defense. I haven't seen that since high school."

Former Louisiana State University coach Dale Brown introduced what he called the "freak defense" in the late 1970s. It was a hybrid defense that combined man-to-man principles with zone principles. Brown used it successfully both in high school and college, and he believed it was the most overlooked defensive technique in the game.

In the freak defense, Brown had his defenders set up in a 1-2-2 alignment and then gave them certain clues; for example, if the entry pass was made to the right side of the court, the defense stayed in the 1-2-2 zone the entire possession. If the entry pass was made to the left side of the court, the defense went man-to-man, and if the first pass was made into the high post, the defense was in a 1-3-1 zone. To make it even more challenging for the opponent, Brown developed a "single clue flip-flop," which meant the clues had changed. He would make this call during a time-out. When the players returned to the court, instead of playing a 1-2-2 zone when the entry pass was made to the right side, the defense was in a 1-3-1 zone. A pass to the high post now resulted in a 1-2-2 zone defense, and an entry pass to the left side of the court dictated a man-to-man defense. Brown upset many ranked teams using his "freak defense," and he thought it was the greatest equalizer of talent that he had ever seen.

Defending Against Out-of-Bounds Plays

The defensive team must be extremely alert when the offensive team is throwing the ball inbounds from either the sideline or the baseline. Too often, one defender relaxes for a second, which allows the offensive team to score an easy basket. All five defenders must communicate and call out screens. It is also important to guard the inbounds passer with active hands so that you can create a turnover.

Diagram 8.43 shows the location of the defense when the ball is taken out from under the basket. The defenders are positioned on the floor in the same spots as though there had been a shot attempted. In other words, the elbows and blocks rebounding rule goes into effect.

Diagram 8.44 shows the defensive positioning when the ball is thrown in from the sideline. All defenders face the ball and remain in their basic 2-3 zone defense.

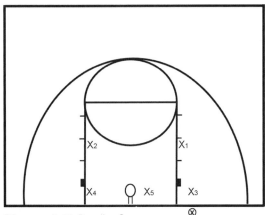

Diagram 8.43 Baseline Coverage

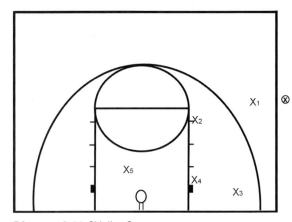

Diagram 8.44 Sideline Coverage

9

Zone Offensive Concepts

The best way to become an excellent zone offensive coach is to become knowledgeable of the defensive slides of the various zones. Unfortunately, very few coaches do this. As a result, most teams' zone offense is far inferior to their man-to-man offense.

At the advent of changing defenses, many coaches believed it was absolutely necessary for their players to recognize the type of zone defense they were facing before they began their attack. Players were more focused on identifying the alignment of the defensive players than attacking the basket and scoring points.

Any time the zone offense is in a "probe mentality" rather than an "attack mode," it helps the defense. This happened in the 2004 Olympics when Team USA overpassed looking for the "sure shot" and ended up taking hurried shots as the shot clock expired.

The purpose of Chapter 9 is to provide the zone offensive concepts that will defeat any type of zone defense. No longer will players take valuable seconds off the shot clock studying the defensive alignment or looking over to the bench asking what zone offense they should be using. Our fundamentally sound and time-tested concepts will enable coaches to design effective zone offenses that will change the mind-set of their players so they are attacking zone defenses with optimism and confidence.

The Quick Break

The single most effective technique available for combating zone defenses is the fast break, also referred to as the quick break. Advancing the ball quickly puts pressure on the zone defenders because they have to sprint back on defense. Over the course of the game, the effectiveness of the half-court zone defense lessens because the defenders are tired and do not react as quickly.

Cam Henderson introduced this concept soon after he created the first zone defense in 1914. He strongly believed the easiest way to score points was to have an outnumbering situation, and the best means to accomplish this was with the quick break. Henderson's desired style of play did not permit the zone defenders to set up in their desired positions and wait for the offensive team.

Hall of Fame coach Clair Bee recognized the brilliance of Henderson during the 1930s and identified the quick break as one of the most important factors in determining team success against a zone defense. This theory still remains true in modern basketball because the quick break limits your opponent's ability to offensively rebound, creates outnumbering situations, and provides excellent opportunities to get the ball into the red zone.

Reduces an Opponent's Second-Shot Opportunities

Teams that always look to fast break against the zone defense reduce the number of second-shot opportunities for their opponents. When preparing to face a fast-breaking team, coaches always stress the importance of getting back on defense, and it usually becomes a dominant theme in the game plan. Some coaches emphasize it so much that it takes away from their team's offensive rebounding. Their players will be running back on defense rather than crashing the offensive boards. This alone gives the fast-breaking team a significant advantage.

Creates Outnumbering Situations

Another reason that fast breaking against a zone defense is paramount for success is because it creates outnumbering situations for the offensive team. As a general rule, defenders do not like to sprint back on defense. It is a period in the game that players like to catch their breath. Consequently, teams that fast break often generate wide-open shots for their players.

Provides Opportunities to Get the Ball into the Red Zone

The third advantage of the fast break is that it creates opportunities to get the ball into the box and elbow areas, called the "red zone." These areas were discussed in Chapter 4 and are the most important spots on the floor for offensive success. The sideline break is popular in international basketball because it forces defenders to drop to the level of the ball, which makes it easier to get the ball into the red zone. Diagram 9.1 shows offense filling the lanes on the primary break and the pass to the post player (4) at the strong side block.

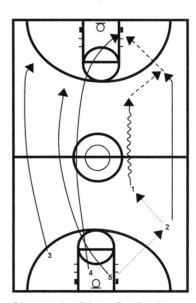

Diagram 9.1 Primary Fast Break

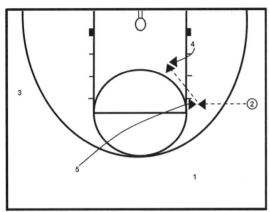

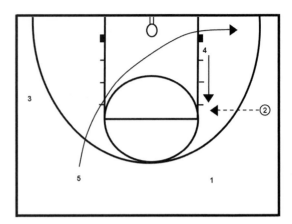

Diagram 9.2 Secondary Fast Break (Option #1)   **Diagram 9.3** Secondary Fast Break (Option #2)

Diagram 9.2 shows a secondary break with the trailer (5) sliding into the elbow area. The offense now has players at both the block and the elbow. When the ball is passed to the elbow, 5 looks for the open shot or the pass into 4.

Diagram 9.3 illustrates another secondary break option for the trailer (5). Instead of sliding into the elbow area, 5 cuts to the short corner. The strong side post (4) breaks up to the elbow. When the ball is passed to the elbow, 4 can shoot, pass to 5 cutting to the basket, or throw a crosscourt pass to 3.

Shot Selection

Knowing when not to shoot is just as important as knowing when to shoot. One of the more difficult tasks of a coach is teaching shot discipline. Coaches must assist players in learning their shooting ranges by keeping accurate statistics and charting shooting drills. Players should adhere to the following guidelines for shooting:

- Be within your shooting range.
- Be well balanced and have a good look at the basket.
- Make sure no other teammate has a better shot.

- Be sure the score and time indicate a need for this shot.
- Check that the rebounding areas are covered.

Offensive Rebounding

One of the best ways to beat a zone defense is to get more than one shot at the basket on every possession. It is wrong to assume that players will naturally secure enough offensive rebounds to win games without a well-conceived plan. Coaches must establish a concrete plan that designates specific responsibilities for each player on every shot attempt. This cannot be emphasized enough because it usually determines the difference between a good season and a great season.

The Box-Plus-One Rebounding Rule

The "box-plus-one" rule is the precursor for offensive rebounding success. Longtime NBA coach Del Harris developed this theory and called it the 2-2-1 offensive rebounding plan. Harris insisted that five areas be filled every time the ball is shot. As shown in Diagram 9.4, letter A designates the safety area; B and C are the boxes; and D and E represent the elbow areas.

The point guard normally fills the safety spot (Area A) and protects against the long pass. Players 2, 3, 4, and 5 fill the areas closest to them when the shot is taken. The only exception would be if the point guard drives to the basket or is positioned on the baseline. When this occurs, the off-guard (2) must read the situation and become the safety.

The key to the box-plus-one rule is that four offensive players

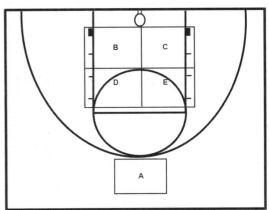

Diagram 9.4 Box-Plus-One Rebounding Areas

Players must attack the offensive boards and assume that all shots will be missed.

must aggressively attack the boards. They are trying to secure the rebound or at least touch the ball and keep it alive so that one of their teammates can retrieve the ball. Going hard to the boards must be enforced every day in practice so that it becomes a habit. Too often, only one offensive rebounder goes to the boards while three players watch the action to see if the shot is missed. By that time, it is too late.

The players filling the elbow areas are very important rebounders. They must assume that every shot will be missed and go to the offensive boards aggressively. They will get a lot of rebounds because opposing players have a difficult time blocking them out when they can get a running start to the basket.

Attacking the Gaps

All zone defensive alignments create gaps between the defensive players. Diagrams 9.5 and 9.6 illustrate the gaps in the 2-1-2 zone and the 1-3-1 zone respectively. Gaps, also referred to as seams, represent the

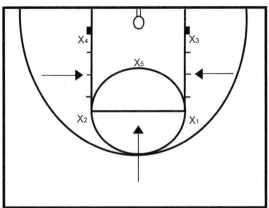

Diagram 9.5 Gaps in a 2-1-2 Zone

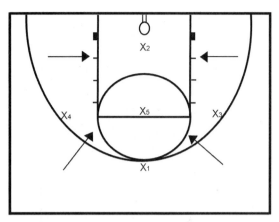

Diagram 9.6 Gaps in a 1-3-1 Zone

weak areas of a zone defense. Smart zone offensive players quickly identify the gaps and know how to attack these areas.

Penetrate-and-Pitch

An important premise in zone offense is: the larger the gap, the more vulnerable the zone defense. A quick penetrating dribble into a gap often results in two defenders converging toward the dribbler. This creates an offensive advantage because it increases the size of an adjacent gap and forces one defensive player to guard two offensive players.

Travis Diener (#34) attacks the seam and has two defenders converging toward him.

Travis Diener (#34) creates an open shot for Todd Townsend (#1) by "freezing" the defensive guard.

Diagram 9.7 shows the penetrate-and-pitch tactic against the 2-1-2 zone defense.

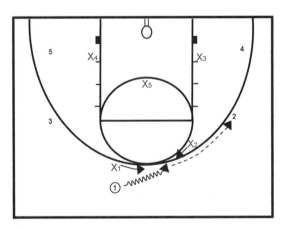

Diagram 9.7 Penetrate-and-Pitch

- The ball handler (1) takes two hard dribbles at X_2. 1's intent is "freeze the defender," which in this case is X_2. It is important that 1 does not go too far into the gap because this will take away the passing lane to 2.
- 1 passes to 2 at the wing.
- X_3 is forced to defend two players (2 and 4).

Odd-Versus-Even Theory

Another way to gain an advantage against a zone defense is to position the offensive players in the gaps when you begin your offense. This will immediately distort the zone defense and take the defenders away from their desired positions.

Diagram 9.8 shows the offensive team in a 2-3 initial formation against the 1-2-2 zone. Many coaches call this the "odd-versus-even" theory, which means if the defense has an odd-player front

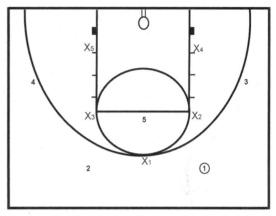

Diagram 9.8 Position Players in the Gaps

(1-2-2, 1-3-1, 3-2), the offense must have an even-player front, such as a 2-3. If the defense has an even-player front (2-1-2, 2-3), the offense should be in an odd-player front, such as a 1-3-1. Implementation of this school of thought immediately forces the defenders to shift from their starting positions.

The authors believe that the odd-versus-even theory is very sound, but it doesn't always have to be accomplished by placing players in the gaps in the initial alignment. Many times it works best to set up in the same alignment as the defense and then send cutters through in order to distort the zone.

Diagram 9.9 shows a 2-3 offensive set attacking a 2-3 zone defense. Initially the offense is matched up with the defensive alignment, but the offensive attack soon becomes a 1-3-1 by sending a cutter to the corner.

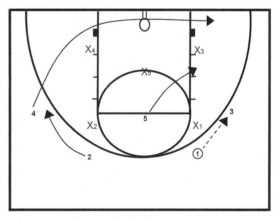

Diagram 9.9 Send Cutter to the Corner

- 1 passes to 3.
- 4 cuts through to the strong side short corner.
- 5 slides down to the side post.
- 2 "spots up" on the weak side wing.

Attack from Behind

Based on the premise that "it is difficult to defend against something you cannot see," it is most effective to attack a zone defense from behind. Having a baseline player, or someone positioned behind the zone, cut to an open area is usually successful because the defenders cannot see the movement of the cutter until it is too late.

Find the "Windows of the Zone"

An important teaching phrase for cutters is to find the "windows of the zone." This means that an offensive player should see a gap and then cut into the opening. This requires patience. Cutters should let the ball be reversed first and then cut to the open area. Many cutters "mirror the ball," which means they move on every pass. When doing this, they are simply moving with the defenders, and it is difficult for them to find an opening.

Two Low Offense

"Two low" is an offense founded on the "attack from behind" principle. It is very effective against a 2-3 zone. The perimeter players (1, 2, and 3) should stay approximately 15 to 18 feet from each other. The inside players (4 and 5) are initially positioned below the block.

Diagram 9.10 shows the pass from the point guard (1) to the wing (2).

- The purpose of the first pass is to make the defenders move and adjust their coverage.
- It is important that both 4 and 5 stay low.
- The perimeter players maintain their proper spacing.
- 3 is prepared for the cross-court pass.
- 2 can take one quick dribble toward the baseline in order to drag X_1 lower and create a larger gap.

Diagram 9.11 illustrates the reverse pass from 2 to 1.

- The strong side post (4) makes a hard cut to the open area at the elbow.
- 5 maintains the same position below the weak side block.
- 2 and 3 "spot up" and are looking for a pass.

Diagram 9.12 shows the pass from 1 to 4. This creates a situation where the weak side post defender (X_4) must defend two players (5 and 3).

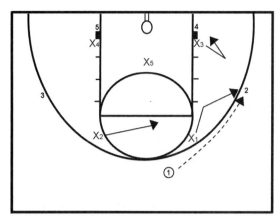

Diagram 9.10 Two Low Offense: Pass to the Wing

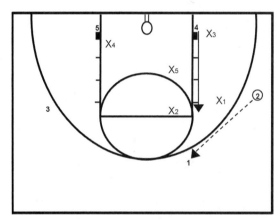

Diagram 9.11 Two Low Offense: Pass Back to the Point

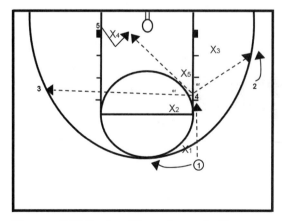

Diagram 9.12 Two Low Offense: Pass to the Elbow

- 4 has the following options:
  a) pass inside to 5; b) shoot
  the elbow jump shot;
  c) throw a crosscourt pass
  to 3 for an open perimeter
  shot; or pass to either 1 or 2
  spotting up on the
  perimeter.

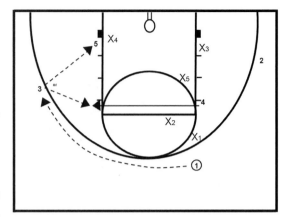

Diagram 9.13 Two Low Offense: Pass to the Weak Side Wing

If 4 is not open at the elbow, the ball should be passed from 1 to the weak side wing (3). (See Diagram 9.13.) This pass puts tremendous pressure on the post defender, X_4.

- 3 looks inside to 5.
- If 5 is not open, 3 looks for the perimeter shot or a pass to 4 cutting to the elbow.

Overload

In a zone defense, players are assigned to cover a specific area. Whenever there is more than one offensive player in a defender's designated area, it creates problems for a zone defense. This offensive strategy is called the "overload principle." In this section, we will discuss the diamond overload set and the swinging overload offense.

Diamond Overload Set

Don Beck, a highly successful coach in the German First League, developed a zone offense that he calls the "diamond overload." Beck has coached the last 14 seasons in two European professional leagues. Prior to going overseas, he coached at Rutgers University and Fresno State.

Air Force creates an overload by placing #45 in the short corner, #21 at the elbow, and #15 at the wing.

Beck adheres to Clair Bee's belief that successful zone offenses attack the weakest areas of the defense. Beck's diamond overload set is based on getting the ball to the elbow and the short corner on the strong side. Diagram 9.14 illustrates these two areas.

About eight years ago, Beck began working with a diamond overload set and found it to be very effective against the standard 2-3 and 3-2 zones used in Europe. It forced the defenders to

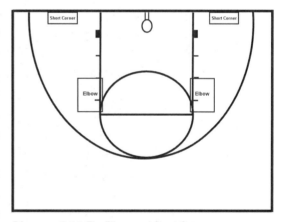

Diagram 9.14 The Elbow and Short Corner

make tough decisions about who should cover the wing, short corner, and high post on the strong side of the court. Basically, it puts a lot of pressure on the back line of any standard 2-3, 3-2, or 1-2-2 zone defensive alignment.

Before going into the basic principles of the diamond overload, it is important for the reader to be aware that the international game uses a 24-second shot clock, not a 35-second clock, and has a time limit of only eight seconds to advance the ball into the frontcourt, not 10 seconds.

Basic Principles. There are five basic principles in Beck's diamond overload set.

1. *Don't stop running.* It is essential to attack the zone defense as quickly as possible. Nothing is more disturbing to Beck than to see teams stop running against a zone defense or initiate their zone offense with two or three meaningless passes. He believes the best way to defeat a zone is to advance the ball quicker than the defenders can get back.

2. *Get to the zone spots quickly.* One of the goals of the diamond overload set is to be able to get into the offense from any- where in the frontcourt with one pass. The standard zone spots in this zone offense can be filled quickly using any standard fast-break attack. Beck utilizes a sideline break, which he feels provides a quick transition from his fast break into his half-court zone offense.

3. *Get a high percentage shot every possession.* The location of the zone spots in the diamond overload presents immediate scoring opportunities, especially if you attack the back line of the defense. Beck encourages his players to take the first good shot available. He believes it is important for your players to understand what defines a "good shot" and have the green light to take that shot.

4. *If you don't have an open shot, reverse the ball.* Beck's offense overloads the zone defense quickly. If there are no scoring opportunities immediately available, the ball is reversed and the zone spots are now established on the newly created strong side. The techniques used to reverse the ball are perimeter passing, dribbling, and inside-outside action.

The type of defense employed by the opponent and how the ball is reversed dictates the subsequent cutting action of the players.

5. *Look to attack off ball reversal.* As the ball is reversed, the players are always looking for scoring opportunities. With the offense being limited by the 24-second clock, the chance for more than one ball reversal is rare. Beck believes his diamond overload set provides multiple opportunities to score within the 24-second time frame. Through the years, Beck has successfully incorporated ball screens, back screens, weak side lob passes, and kick-outs in his diamond overload set.

Scoring Options. Diagram 9.15 illustrates all the spots in the diamond overload set. The spots are located at the wing, elbow, short corner, and guard position. The short corner spots are located approximately half the distance between the baskets and corners. The player who fills the short corner should have his or her heels as close as possible to the baseline. The guard spots are located beyond the three-point line, approximately 15 to 18 feet apart, and are parallel to the short corner spots. The elbow spot is very important and should be the last position filled.

Diagram 9.16 shows the initial alignment of the diamond overload and the pass from the guard (1) to the wing (3). The wing (3)

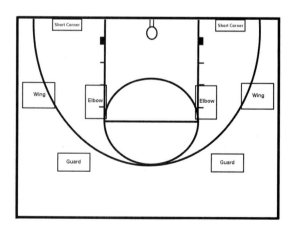

Diagram 9.15 Diamond Overload Spots

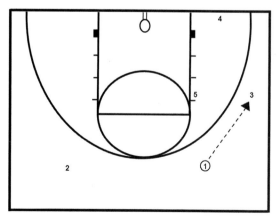

Diagram 9.16 Pass from the Guard to the Wing

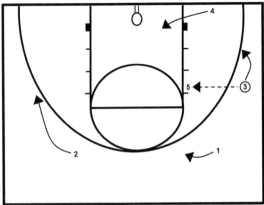

Diagram 9.17 Pass from the Wing to the Elbow

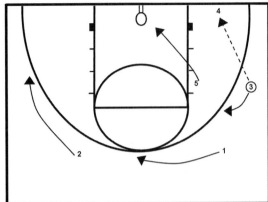

Diagram 9.18 Pass from the Wing to the Short Corner

immediately looks to the elbow (5) and the short corner (4). If either player is open, the pass must be thrown. The importance of getting the ball to the elbow or the short corner cannot be overemphasized.

Diagram 9.17 shows 5 receiving the pass at the strong side elbow. He or she immediately faces the basket and looks for 4 cutting into the alley.

Diagram 9.18 shows 4 receiving the pass in the short corner and immediately looking for 5 cutting toward the basket.

If the wing (3) is unable to pass to either 5 or 4, the ball is passed back to the guard (1), who immediately looks inside to 5. If that option is not open, 5 can set a screen for 1. Diagram 9.19 shows 1 using the screen and looking for the best scoring opportunity. These options include taking the perimeter shot, passing to either wing, or throwing a lob pass to 4.

Diagram 9.20 shows the cutting action when the ball is passed to the wing (2) and the overload is swung to the opposite side of the floor. It is very important that 2 dribbles away from the baseline to create the proper spacing. The

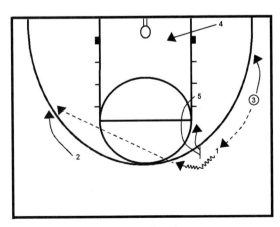

Diagram 9.19 Screen for the Guard

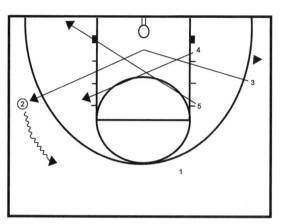

Diagram 9.20 Cutting Action

forward (3) cuts into the lane and then breaks out to the wing. The high post (5) cuts toward the baseline to the short corner spot, and 4 flashes up to the strong side elbow. The diamond overload is now established on the opposite side of the floor.

The Swinging Overload Offense

Coauthor Pim designed a zone offense at Central Michigan based on the zone offensive concepts of Dr. Tom Davis and the strengths and weaknesses of Central's personnel. The offense is called the "swinging overload" and is similar to Beck's diamond overload set, because the overload shifts to the strong side when the ball is reversed.

The offense was initially developed to maximize the talents of a post player who was an outstanding offensive rebounder but a very poor perimeter shooter. Most of our opponents did not guard this player outside the confines of the lane, so we often had four offensive players trying to beat five defenders. To combat this, we created a continuity zone offense keeping our post player in the backside rebounding area the majority of the time.

Diagram 9.21 shows the initial alignment of the swinging overload. The post player (5) starts in the high post, while 3 and 4 are aligned in a stack on the weak side of the floor.

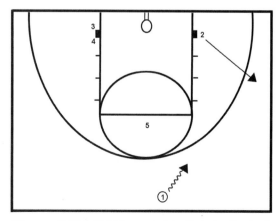

Diagram 9.21 Initial Alignment of the Swinging Overload

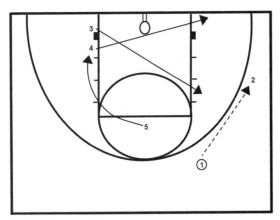

Diagram 9.22 Pass to the Wing

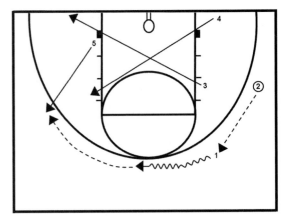

Diagram 9.23 Ball Reversal

Diagram 9.22 shows the ball being passed from 1 to 2. The high post (5) goes to the backside rebounding spot, 3 cuts to the elbow, and 4 goes to the short corner on the strong side of the court. The zone offense now has the same options that were described in Beck's diamond overload set.

Diagram 9.23 shows the movement of the players when the ball is reversed. The low post (5) cuts to the wing for the pass. As 5 receives the ball, 3 cuts to the short corner and 4 makes a flash cut to the strong side. The diamond overload is now created on the opposite side of the floor.

When 5 passes the ball (to the short corner, elbow, or guard), he or she immediately cuts to the backside rebounding spot, and 1 fills the wing position in the overload. (See Diagram 9.24.)

The swinging overload is an example of an offense that was built on the strengths and weaknesses of a team's personnel. There are endless opportunities for creative coaches who want to maximize their talent.

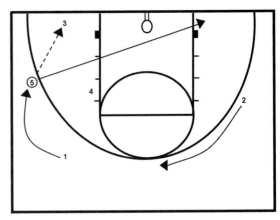

Diagram 9.24 Pass to the Short Corner

Rotation

Rotating players into the vulnerable areas of a zone defense can be very productive because it provides a way for your best players to receive the ball in an area of the floor that showcases their talents.

Diagram 9.25 shows an option that the Cleveland Cavaliers use to create scoring opportunities for LeBron James. On the pass from 1 to 3, James (2) slips into the elbow area. When James receives the ball at the elbow, he is positioned to have multiple scoring options for himself and his teammates.

Diagram 9.26 shows 1 dribbling to the wing and looking for an entry pass to 5 at the midpost area. At the same time, 2 loops down to the baseline, and 4 breaks to the top of the circle.

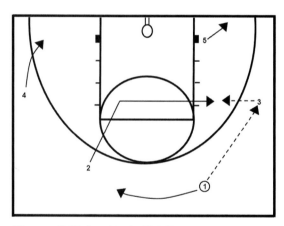

Diagram 9.25 Guard to the High Post

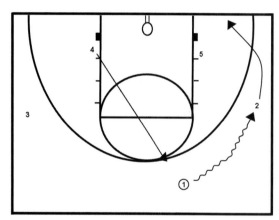

Diagram 9.26 Dribble to the Wing

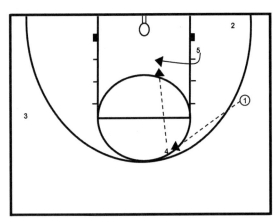

Diagram 9.27 Kick-Back Pass

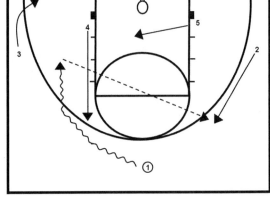

Diagram 9.28 Diagonal Pass

Diagram 9.27 shows the kick-back pass from 1 to 4 and the high-low pass from 4 to 5. It is important that the post player (4) has one foot inside the top of the circle so that the high-low pass can be made quicker.

Diagram 9.28 illustrates the diagonal pass from 1 to 2, which is an excellent option for a kick-out pass and shot. When the point guard (1) turns the corner on dribble penetration, 4 loops out, 5 flashes to the post area, 3 moves to the corner, and 2 lines up with the ball handler and creates a diagonal passing angle. It is important that 2 meets the pass and has his or her hands ready to shoot.

Summary

The authors hope that Chapter 9 has stimulated your zone offensive thinking. Because of the wide variation in zone defenses, it is impossible to provide answers for all the problems that may arise. That is your responsibility as a coach. The zone offensive concepts that have been presented should serve as a foundation, but your philosophy and personal preferences based on the talents of your players will dictate your success. Study zone defenses, be creative in your approach when attacking them, and spend practice time developing the skills of your players.

Appendix

As the authors hope this book has demonstrated, the history and proper execution of the zone have both hinged on a team's ability to adapt. Each successful coach puts his or her fingerprints on the systems described, discovering new techniques within common structures. The following list of coaches have in some way made their mark with the zone, either using it or attacking it. These coaches represent some of the best the world has seen at every level. We encourage you to explore their work. The games they have coached are by all standards "recommended reading," and we believe by doing a Google search, viewing footage of their classic games, or studying their publications, you will further develop your own ability to own the zone and make it work for you.

CLAIR BEE One of basketball's greatest teachers and strategists. This Hall of Fame coach was decades ahead of his time.

VALERIO BIANCHINI This Italian coach is both a teacher and tactician; he helped develop Brian Shaw and Danny Ferry.

JIM BOEHEIM His 2-3 at Syracuse is part of the Orange tradition, one strong enough to win the 2003 NCAA championship.

VIC BUBAS This legendary Duke coach was a true visionary.

JOHN CALIPARI Currently with Memphis, he constantly beat John Chaney's match-up at Temple while at UMass.

ROY CHIPMAN This Pitt coach deserves recognition because of his high 1-3-1 zone and use of trapping back.

CHUCK DALY A former Penn and Olympic coach, Daly won the NBA championship with the Detroit Pistons.

TOM DAVIS He may have run the most used zone offense in the world. His point drop zone from a 1-2-2 set has merit today.

LEFTY DRIESELL From Maryland, his double-low wreaked havoc against the zone.

JOHN EGLI Author of the classic book *Sliding Zone Defenses for Winning Basketball*.

JIM FOSTER His early use of the triangle-and-two was very effective.

SANDRO GAMBA He brought Italian basketball to the world scene.

PINHAS GERSHON Known for his game management skills.

PANAGIOTIS GIANNAKIS His innovative style defeated Team USA at the Tokyo World Games in 2006.

ALEXANDER GOMELSKY The father of modern basketball in the former Soviet Union. A 1988 Gold Medal winner.

BILL GREEN Played the ultimate match-up with a rover to a record six Indiana state titles—ingenious.

MARV HARSHMAN This former University of Washington coach had great set concepts versus zones/match-up.

JUD HEATHCOTE Won NCAA for Michigan State (with Magic Johnson) using his match-up.

CAM HENDERSON Inventor of the zone defense in 1914. His innovative mind revolutionized the game.

JOSÉ VICENTE "PEPU" HERNÁNDEZ He won gold in Tokyo in 2006. Known as a "quick-break" coach.

DUSKO IVANOVIC Ivanovich is another product of the rich basketball region surrounding the former Yugoslavia.

DUSAN IVKOVIC This Serbian coach has been a head coach in Euroleague since 1980.

JONAS KAZLAUSKAS This former coach of the Lithuanian national team is currently China's head coach for the 2008 Olympics.

BOB KNIGHT Coach Knight goes for the gaps against the zone better than anyone.

JACK KRAFT Take a look at this former Villanova coach's "ball defense"; it hasn't been seen for a while.

MIKE KRZYZEWSKI Years of excellence across the game. Outside of his program at Duke, he also coached Team USA.

JOHN LAWTHER Creator of the sliding zone defense.

HARRY LITWACK Don Casey's mentor from Temple. He had the match-up before anyone.

JACK MCCLOSKEY McCloskey exposed the Big 5 and ACC to "Penn State slides."

ETTORE MESSINA Won several Euroleague trophies.

KEN NORTON Used the clock offense against zones to success.

MIRKO NOVOSEL A great match-up coach and Hall of Famer.

ZELIMIR OBRADOVIC Serbian coach and practitioner of the Eastern European style.

DAVE ODOM Many say his zone offense is one of the best around.

LUTE OLSON Runs solid match-up zone rules, and his tactics against the zone are sound and effective.

DAN PETERSON This excellent tactician coached several European and Italian championships.

RICK PITINO Currently with Louisville, one word describes Pitino's full court zone match-up press—"awesome."

JACK RAMSAY Master of the 2-2-1 set against the zone, attacked through the middle, not the edges.

BUZZ RIDL and FRAN WEBSTER The "amoeba" defensive gurus.

DEE ROWE Ran a very effective "stack set" against zones.

DEAN SMITH Taking a look at the Carolina "Point Zone" is definitely worth your while.

BOB WEINHAUER This Final Four coach gave Temple's zone fits.

PAUL WESTHEAD His system against the zone, represented by his "break-break" motto, made it difficult for his opponents.

MORGAN WOOTTEN DeMatha High School coach with over 1,000 wins. Read everything he has written!

Bibliography

Adams, Ron. *A Man-to-Man Pressure Defense System*. Fresno, Calif.: California State University, 1981.

Baisi, Neal. *Coaching the Zone and Man-to-Man Pressing Defenses*. Englewood Cliffs, N.J.: Prentice-Hall, 1961.

Bee, Clair. *The Science of Coaching*. New York: A. S. Barnes, 1942.

———. *Zone Defense and Attack*. New York: A. S. Barnes, 1942.

Casey, Don. *The Temple of Zones II*. San Diego, Calif., 1984.

Clagg, Sam. *The Cam Henderson Story*. Parsons, W.V.: McClain Printing, 1981.

Crean, Tom, and Ralph Pim. *Coaching Team Basketball*. New York: McGraw-Hill, 2007.

DeCourcy, Mike. "Foes Find It Easy to Zone Out vs. Temple." *The Sporting News*, January 8, 1996.

Egli, John. *The Sliding Zone Defense for Winning Basketball*. West Nyack, N.Y.: Parker Publishing, 1970.

Enlund, Tom. "Karl Reluctantly Changing the Way His Team Plays Defense." *Milwaukee Journal Sentinel*, November 19, 2002.

Fraschilla, Fran. "Changes Needed for U.S. to Succeed Internationally." ESPN.com, August 22, 2005. http://proxy.espn.go.com/espn/print?id=2140171&type=story.

Green, Bill. *Bill Green's Match-Up Zone Defense*. St. Cloud, Minn.: Let's Teach Basketball, 1978.

Harris, Del. *Winning Defense*. Indianapolis, Ind.: Masters Press, 1993.

Hu, Janny. "Nellie Points to Better Defense." *San Francisco Chronicle*, October 10, 2006.

Jenkins, Bruce. *A Good Man: The Pete Newell Story*. Berkeley, Calif.: Frog, Ltd., 1999.

Katz, Andy. "Longtime Temple Coach Wants to Stay Awhile." ESPN.com, September 21, 2005. http://sports.espn.go.com/espn/print?id=2167838&type=story.

Keogan, George E. "A Defense for the Figure 8 Offense." *The Athletic Journal* (December 1934).

Knight, Bob, with Bob Hammel. *Knight: My Story*. New York: Thomas Dunne Books, 2002.

Krause, Jerry, Don Meyer, and Jerry Meyer. *Basketball Skills and Drills.* Champaign, Ill.: Human Kinetics, 1999.

Krause, Jerry, and Ralph Pim. *Basketball Defense.* Monterey, Calif.: Coaches Choice, 2005.

———. *Coaching Basketball.* Chicago: Contemporary Books, 2002.

Lawther, George. "My Dad, the Coach." *The Pilot* newspaper, December 14, 2003.

McCloskey, Jack. Interview by Don Casey and Ralph Pim, April 8, 2007.

McCosky, Chris. "Wallace Hates Zone Defense." *The Detroit News,* October 5, 2006.

Meanwell, Walter E. *The Science of Basketball.* Madison, Wis.: Democrat Publishing, 1924.

Meyer, Don. *PAT—Point and Talk Match-Up Man Defense.* Notes from Don Meyer Basketball Camps, Nashville, Tenn., 2006.

———. "The Buoy from Syracuse." *Coach and Athletic Director,* September 2003.

Olson, Lute. *Arizona Pressure Defense.* Tucson, Ariz.: University of Arizona, 1983.

Pim, Ralph. *Winning Basketball.* New York: McGraw-Hill, 2004.

Ramsay, Jack. *Dr. Jack's Leadership Lessons Learned from a Lifetime in Basketball.* Hoboken, N.J.: John Wiley & Sons, 2004.

———. *Pressure Basketball.* Englewood Cliffs, N.J.: Prentice-Hall, 1963.

Raveling, George. *War on the Boards.* Mt. Pocono, Penn.: Athletic Technologists, 1972.

Rowe, James. "Defensive Drills vs. Penetration and the Pick and Roll." *Coach and Athletic Director,* October 2002.

Smith, Dean, John Kilgo, and Sally Jenkins. *A Coach's Life.* New York: Random House, 2002.

Thomsen, Ian. "Time for Offenses to Start Adjusting: The Zone Defense Rules." *Sports Illustrated,* December 15, 2003.

Waters, Mike. "Inside the Syracuse Zone." *The Sporting News,* September 29, 2003.

Webster, Fran. *Basketball's Amoeba Defense.* West Nyack, N.Y.: Parker Publishing, 1984.

Wolff, Alexander. "Danger Zone." *Sports Illustrated,* March 16, 1998.

Wootten, Morgan. *Coaching Basketball Successfully.* Champaign, Ill.: Human Kinetics, 2003.

"Zoned Out—College Basketball Notebook." MSNBC.com, February 19, 2005. http://www.msnbc.msn.

Index

About the Authors

DON CASEY has taught the principles of zone defense around the world, working with athletes in Beirut, Johannesburg, Berlin, Haiti, Ecuador, Bosnia-Herzegovina, and Taiwan.

His first coaching assignment came at the age of 20 at Bishop Eustace Preparatory School in Pennsauken, New Jersey, as the head basketball coach, where he won two New Jersey state basketball championships. He was the head coach of Temple University from 1973 through 1982 and led the Owls to an outstanding winning percentage of .616. He showed his progressive thinking by taking his squad to Tokyo, Japan, to play UCLA in the first NCAA game played on foreign soil. It was during his collegiate coaching years that he authored *The Temple of Zones*, a book featuring diagrams on how to play an effective zone defense.

Following his successful reign at Temple, Casey joined the NBA's Chicago Bulls for the 1982–83 campaign as an assistant under Paul Westhead and had the same title with Jimmy Lynam and the Clippers the following season. In 1984–85, Casey's next coaching stop took him to Italy. He rejoined the Clippers as an assistant to both Don Chaney and Gene Shue for the next three-plus seasons until replacing Shue as head coach January 19, 1989, for the balance of that season and all of the 1989–90 season.

He was the lead assistant coach to Chris Ford for five seasons and M. L. Carr for one during his six seasons with the Boston Celtics from 1990 to 1996. Casey was John Calipari's lead assistant with the Nets for the 1996–97 and 1997–98 seasons. Following a 3–17 start in 1998–99, Casey was promoted to head coach, and the Nets rebounded with a 13–17 mark for the balance of that abridged season and for the entire 1999–2000 season. He was also the Vice Chairman of the President's Council on Physical Fitness and Sports for much of the 1990s, and most recently worked with Team USA on zone concepts.

The genial Casey now lives outside San Diego, California, with his lovely wife, Dwynne. They are the proud parents of Michael, LeeAnn, and Sean and grandparents to Jack Sean Patrick and Alex Joseph.

RALPH PIM is an associate professor and chief of competitive sports in the Department of Physical Education at the United States Military Academy at West Point.

Prior to his arrival at West Point in 2000, Pim served as chairperson of the physical education department and head men's basketball coach at Limestone College (South Carolina). Pim coached basketball at the secondary and collegiate levels for 25 years. As a collegiate head coach, Pim built Alma (Michigan) College and Limestone College into highly successful programs. His Alma teams were ranked nationally for points scored and three-point field goals, and the 1989 squad recorded the school's best overall record in 47 years. He also coached at Central Michigan, William and Mary, Northwestern Louisiana, and Barberton (Ohio) High School. Barberton won the 1976 Ohio State Championship and was selected the seventh best team in the country.

Pim spent 10 years as the technical advisor for the Basketball Association of Wales. He implemented training programs to facilitate the development of basketball throughout the country of Wales. He also assisted with the training of their national teams at the Olympic Training Center in Cardiff, Wales.

Pim has authored seven books on basketball and is a nationally recognized speaker. He has presented during the 2005 Naismith Memorial Basketball Hall of Fame Enshrinement Weekend and at the NCAA Men's Basketball Final Four from 2004 through 2007.

A native of Akron, Ohio, Pim is a graduate of Springfield College (Massachusetts). He earned his master's degree from Ohio State University and his doctorate from Northwestern Louisiana State University. Pim is a member of the Phi Kappa Phi honor society. At West Point, Pim received the Brigadier General James L. Anderson Award for excellence in teaching in 2005. He serves on the national committee for the Champions of Character for the National Association of Intercollegiate Athletics. Pim was inducted into the Limestone College Athletic Hall of Fame in 2007 and introduced the Mike Krzyzewski Teaching Character Through Sport Award at West Point in 2007.